Toward Community

A Post-Shoah Christian Theology

James F. Moore

Studies in the Shoah

Volume XXVII

University Press of America,® Inc.
Dallas · Lanham · Boulder · New York · Oxford

Copyright © 2004 by
University Press of America,® Inc.
4501 Forbes Boulevard
Suite 200
Lanham, Maryland 20706
UPA Acquisitions Department (301) 459-3366

PO Box 317
Oxford
OX2 9RU, UK

Library of Congress Control Number: 2003117054
ISBN 0-7618-2836-2 (paperback : alk. ppr.)

To Joe and Barbara for their support and inspiration

Table of Contents

Preface

This project began 10 years ago with the model that I set out in *Christian Theology after the Shoah*. That model was an argument for a Christian theology that can be genuine only if it is at the same time done in dialogue, especially with Jews, and done as a post-Shoah theology. No theology, I claimed, could be authentic unless that theology is post-Shoah. Of course, that book was not a full examination of what such a theology would be. Instead, I chose to give a structure that could be a first step toward making sure that any theologizing would automatically assume fundamental criteria that could judge some statements, no matter how reasonably such statements seem as part of a belief system, as no longer possible to say. Thus the model functions mostly as a negative theology identifying what cannot be said far more than what might be said. A positive theology, that is, one that could provide workable and acceptable positions for a post-Shoah world, must be done in dialogue.

Thus, ten years ago I also organized a dialogue, building on the previous work and a dialogue relationship that was already nearly more than a decade old at that time. That dialogue group (what has become known among those who know of it as the midrash group) included two Jewish scholars and one Christian who joined me in a project of examining sacred texts together. The aim was to bring the criteria of genuine theology to bear on an open conversation about texts, some of which we could believe we shared and others which proved to be new ground for thought for my two Jewish colleagues. The pattern has remained the same over the ten years of our conversations. We have annually thought about and interacted about two texts (one from Hebrew scriptures and one from Christian scriptures) paired in ways that made them corollaries of one another in a general sense. These conversations always presumed three basic presuppositions. First, we would manage our own thinking so as to be open to each other, open to the possibility of surprise. Second, we dedicated our reflections to be post-Shoah asking the hard questions about how the possible meanings we could uncover in our reading of these texts might sound in the ears of the one million children who died – to use Irving Greenberg's central challenge. Third, we agreed that our conversations must be dialogical. That is, we had to find an approach that allowed for a conversation between Jewish thinking and Christian thinking in all of our individual reflections on both texts. That is, we had to introduce a method, one that was already described in my earlier book, a midrashic approach to reading texts.

That conversation has continued without break for the last ten years and has produced a series of publications. The content of those conversations is significant mostly for the dialogical context and the post-Shoah reading. The end point is not necessarily that we have shaped a new theology even though pieces of such a theology might be found in the inter-play between our papers. The end point, as I have come to see more and more, is that the process has created a dialogical community. We have found not only a common language and common values and purposes, but we have also created bonds of connection. This has emerged not so much by plan but as part of the process of meeting and talking over these years.

The chapters in this book represent a collection of inter-linking essays that were written over this same period. In the essays the reader can see that the idea of a dialogical community grows from an implicit notion that is part of early essays toward an explicit idea that increasingly becomes the focus of attention for my reflections. In fact, this forming of community in ways that are not clear (that is, we do not know what lies ahead of us) may well be central to any post-Shoah world, more significant than any positive theological response. Ours is not the only such emerging community, obviously, but the decade of reflection has become an opportunity to explore both what this community is and how it necessarily contributes both to our conversations and to our goals for a different kind of world after the Shoah.

Of course, the essays are mine and the thoughts are my responsibility, but the possibility of carrying on this process of reflection has included many important people who have made the ongoing conversation possible. Among those most helpful have been the various people associated with the Annual Scholars' Conference on the Holocaust and the Churches who have provided a place for our annual dialogues as well as being an audience and co-participants in this discussion. This means, in particular, Franklin and Marci Littell and Hubert Locke who continue to provide important leadership for all of us. Of course, the dialogues were most directly influenced for me by my partners in conversation, Steven Jacobs, Henry Knight and Zev Garber. They are not only exceptionable scholars but have become close friends in a way that only this sort of dialogue could produce. Many in this circle, of course, also joined in our discussions along the way.

My own work has been possible only because of the generosity of my university and department. These colleagues have been understanding and supportive all along the way. One colleague who no longer is part of our department but remains among my closest friends and comrades in dialogue is Joseph Edelheit. His work is an inspiration to me and our ongoing, never-ending interaction, which was the model that gave me the sense of what a dialogue could be, has been a treasure which has made my growth as a part of a Jewish-Christian dialogue possible. I have also had the good fortune to share life with a scholar who not only has been a regular commentator on the midrash group and its work but has had a profound influence on how I see the whole project. Without Barbara Strassberg's insight, I could not have come to understand the dynamics of the growing presence of a community of dialogue. Her input has led me to re-fashion my approach, to make it clearer and to turn the whole dialogue toward concrete, relevant goals that might actually have an impact on people. Of course, as my spouse and friend and partner, she has enriched my life in ways that simply sustain me and allow me to be fresh and ready for every new task with excitement.

I thank all of these people for what they have given me over the years and in some way I hope the essays in this book is also a tribute to their association with me. The following chapters represent a work in progress with much that is still yet to be thought and said. This book is simply an attempt to pause a moment to capture what has happened in this remarkable conversation up to this point.

Acknowledgements

The essay, "The Israel-Shoah Link," first appeared in the *Proceedings of the 22nd Annual Scholars' Conference on the Holocaust*, Lewiston, NY: Edwin Mellon, 1995.

The essay, "Re-Envisioning Christianity," first appeared in *Cross Currents*, volume 50:4, Winter 2000/2001, pp. 437-447.

The essay, "Recovering the European Perspective," first appeared in the *Proceedings of the Sixth Conference of the International Society for the Study of European Ideas*, Haifa, 1998.

All of these essays appear by permission of the publishers.

Chapter One: Choose Life - Reading
Deuteronomy 30:19-20 in a post-Shoah World

Our Dialogue As Model

The discussion that produced the essays in this book is a possible model for the theological framework of a post-Shoah theology. The format I have imposed brings with it several features that make it ideal for the difficult work that post-Shoah theology requires. The make-up of the group of scholars that became my dialogue partners, for example, was specifically chosen to engage in a dialogue that presents a balanced perspective between Christians and Jews. The particular individuals involved also represent distinct perspectives that enrich the conversation between us. The discussion is also well suited to our purpose since it is both possible to give definite shape to our mutual thinking while assuring at the same time a sense of both openness to surprise and creative and productive interaction. Thus the format also implies a sort of openness to the future that the difficult and ever changing discussion in dialogue requires. Indeed, if we could manage such discussions regularly in busy schedules, the conversation format would be an especially inviting model for post-Shoah dialogue. But, the essays in this book presume this dialogue as background for whatever is said.

Therefore, I offer this discussion as a paradigm for post-Shoah theology, especially as that now must be done in the second generation of scholars. It is this kind of setting that, I contend, provides the optimum context for both generating dialogue and testing our conclusions, for creating a viable post-Shoah theology. In addition, the nature of such a discussion suggests that the circle of contributors can and probably must expand. That is, the nature of this dialogue implies that this may also be a model for interaction that involves anyone who is studying seriously the relationship between Christianity and Judaism in this post-Shoah world. Thus, the discussion here can become an example of this interaction applicable to any class on contemporary Judaism and the dialogue itself may well suggest a model for creating this interaction in the classroom. Surely, then the results apply to more than just the shaping of theology but have to do with the nature of and the future shape of contemporary Judaism and Christianity.

The Criteria

There is much about our conversation that requires a certain sense of openness in conversation, readiness, even eagerness to allow for surprises and variety of approach and perspective. We do not want to discourage the flexibility nor the creativity of discussion that a panel represents. Still, there are certain beginning criteria that function as necessary boundaries for our discussion, agreements or groundrules that help provide a framework for beginning our conversation. These rules are fairly self-evident given the goals of our discussion, a post-Shoah theology. They are: (1) that our theology be self-consciously dialogical; (2) that our theology be sensitive to the issues that emerge for religious thought out of the Shoah; (3) that our discussion be theological, that is attending to theological concerns and not primarily other certainly important concerns.

Our theology must be dialogical. Those of us who are practised in dialogue may find this criteria fairly self-evident, but it is nevertheless vital to this approach to post-Shoah theology. That is to say, the point of our work is not merely to settle the parochial questions interesting to our particular group but rather to engage in those questions that have the potential to affect us both and to form some potential common ground. This is a mutual conversation and what we say or choose for our focus requires this ongoing sense of mutuality. On that level dialogue includes at least four critical features: (1) a willingness to listen to the other as other; (2) a willingness to accept as valid the truth commitments of the other; (3) a willingness to explore anew and bring to the conversation the particular perspective that is our own (our own faith perspective)- and (4) a willingness to risk change.' Many have suggested to me that the last of these components of dialogue is really the first, the main commitment. Since there is likely to be a changed viewpoint in some way produced by the conversation (indeed, this may even be the goal of dialogue), a willingness to risk change is required before we begin and not as a potential by-product of the conversation. If this is so, then points 3 and 2 are filled with more than what is at first implied.

Our willingness to bring to the conversation our own faith perspective (and we are talking here of religious dialogue, dialogue on and about the sacred as we experience and come to know and make real in our lives the sacred) already presumes the limits of our personal or communal view. We engage in conversation with the desire to re-think what is our own perspective even if we also come to dialogue with a firm commitment to that perspective and to that faith community. And we must say that the dialogue will produce change but change that is itself both a unique experience to each participant, not to be superficially assumed as the same as one's own, but is also already in the conversation a part of the dialogue. This bringing to the conversation one's own perspective with the willingness to risk change is that which drives the conversation forward toward legitimate surprise. But this means that point two is also deeper than seems at first. We come to the dialogue already prepared to grant the legitimacy of the other's claims. That does not mean mere tolerance as not every claim may in the end be acceptable. Indeed, we expect that our post-Shoah reflections will call some views into question. Even so, our willingness to risk change means that our willingness reaches to the core of our own belief. Now this is risky since we are[1] led to that precarious level of thinking that sees competing claims for truth to be the only viable vehicle by which our dialogue can proceed, either in acceptable directions or in honest acceptance, indeed, inclusion of the other. Once again, we enter with a new level of naivete, a commitment to start again in our thinking about the other. We discard prejudice that is born by our own traditions and begin with this exciting and threatening commitment to accept the other fully. We know that this expanded sense of our willingness to accept the other's views as true gives a richer meaning to the first point as well. We know that our intent in actually listening to the views of another is changed, or at least directed in particular ways. We listen with intent and that intent is shaped by respect and a desire to re-think what we claim is true or believe might be true about ourselves, our world, our God and with that about the other. What ever we might have thought

---

[1] I originally proposed this model for understanding dialogue in:

James Moore, "Team-Taught, In-Class Dialogue: A Limited But Promising Method For Teaching Judaism," in *Methodology in the Academic Teaching of Judaism,* Zev Garber, ed., (Lanham, MD: University Press of America, 1986), p. 202ff.

is true about the other is always open to a new listening, to surprises because we assume that we might be wrong, we might not really have heard before, we might honestly hear something so new and vital that we truly have not considered before. This is what we mean by saying from the outset that our theology must be dialogical.

Our theology must also be post-Shoah. Now there is a way in which our conversation will be necessarily post-Shoah, that is, we are necessarily products of cultures that are sustained in a world that has suffered the impact of the Shoah. We cannot detail here all that might be meant by that statement, but we cannot escape the reality of the Shoah as an historical event which has had enormous impact especially on our two faith communities. But we argue that our conversation must be self-consciously post-Shoah. Johannes Metz has said that no theology can be done now without considering what that theology means in the light of Auschwitz.[2] Irving Greenberg has said that nothing can be said theologically today unless it could be said in the presence of the one million children who died.[3] That is to say, our commitment is not merely the recognition that the historical fact of the Shoah cannot be denied (it is at least that) but means also that our theologies cannot be the same anymore. Our language cannot be naively offered as if Auschwitz had not been. Now we turn to what Elie Wiesel has clearly said. We attempt the impossible in this dialogue since we try through the vehicle of dialogue, through whatever wisdom we can muster, to stand at Auschwitz, to ask the impossible question, "What does it mean that there is a connection between standing at Sinai and standing at Auschwitz, knowing, of course, that none of us stood at Auschwitz?"

This impossible but necessary task will mean something different to every contributor to this conversation. We know that to listen to one another with all eagerness to hear will mean that we discard assumptions about what it means for any of us to think as if we were there, to speak as if those who were already dying could hear us. We do know that we cannot waste this moment with meaningless

---

[2] Johannes Baptist Metz, *The Emergent Church* (New York: Crossroad, 1981), p. 28.
[3] Irving Greenberg, "Cloud of Smoke, Pillar of Fire: Judaism, Christianity, and Modernity after the Holocaust," in *Auschwitz.- Beginning of a New Era?*, Eva Fleischner, ed. (New York: KTAV Publishing House, 1977), p. 13.

chatter even if we fear always that what we say will sound like meaningless chatter. This surely also means that when we speak theologically we will speak with certain questions always in mind. We will ask whether this particular way of talking, of thinking of conceiving ourselves and the other makes sense inside of the Shoah story. And we will know the words well from Wiesel or from Fackenheim that such an effort is hopeless.[4] Nothing makes sense inside of the Shoah story. Even so, we still ask and realize that there is a way to do this. We keep asking always fearful that our theologies will be ruined on the rocks of this task but still knowing that our basic trust, our faith commitment is perhaps the only hope that we will not be broken on the rocks of this task. This is the shape of the bold confidence that mixes with the possibility of utter despair that comes forth with the complete humility that we must surely fail and finishes with the realization that we must succeed and can only in this way succeed. We will know some questions that we share and others that perhaps only we have come to ask. All of these questions, perhaps especially the questions, become our theology. This is what we mean when we say that our theology must be post-Shoah.

Finally, our dialogue must be theological. Of course, there are other disciplines that demand attention in post-Shoah thinking. In fact, our ability to consider a post-Shoah theology now is dependent on much work that has already been done by historians, social scientists, philosophers, and literary critics and creative writers. But, our dialogue must be theological. This means that our conversation will focus on theological themes. The earlier dialogues of our era did not do this in the interest of building a level of trust and mutual concern. Many feared that discussions on theology would threaten dialogue itself and ruin efforts for mutual cooperation. Theological themes are also the most problematic after the Shoah. Fackenheim's question, "Why did they do it?," is at first a moral question but is also the deep theological question, an ultimate question.[5] This question is one that eludes our answers. Thus, early partners in dialogue avoided these questions many times. And these questions, ultimate questions, may

---

[4] cf., Emil Fackenheim, To *Mend the World* (New York: Schocken Books, 1982), p. 230ff.
[5] Emil Fackenheim, "Holocaust and Weltanschauung: Philosophical Reflections as to Why They Did It," in *Remembering for the Future,* YehudaBauer, ed., (New York: Pergamon Press, 1988), volume 2, p. 1850ff.

be the most troubling for those of us who were not there. Eliezer
Berkovitz implies that such questions of morality and religion cannot
be answered fully except by those who were there.[6] Can we judge
whether such answers worked or work even now unless we were there?

But theological matters are now the critical arena for our
dialogue. If we are to heed Wiesel and connect Sinai with Auschwitz,
we cannot do this in any other way except by asking the theological
questions. But this means, of course, that our theology must connect
Sinai with Auschwitz. Thus, pre-Shoah theologies cannot be our
theologies until they have been sifted through the sieve of the Shoah.
This is all the more reason for saying that our dialogue must be
theological. This connecting of basic tradition with current questions
is what we have always meant by theology. This hermeneutical task is
the theological task. This search for meaning between text and
context, between Sinai and Auschwitz is the theological search.
Anyone who seeks to ask such questions enters into this theological
discussion whether they are theologians or not, but the quest is a
theological quest that follows theological instincts. And the arena we
have been describing is what we mean by a dialogue that is
theological.

The Focus of Our Discussion

We must have a beginning point of course. Various kinds of
entrees into reflection on the Shoah can take a beginning from a
variety of different places -- the historical facts, the stories of survivors
and victims, the case studies of sociologists or psychologists -- but a
theology begins within our traditions. To ask the theological questions
that we must ask requires that we ask them of our sacred texts. We
begin with the sacred text as all theologies do. Of course, we begin
with the sacred text inside the framework we have already described.
We approach the sacred text in dialogue and all that we have agreed
that means. We read the sacred texts from a post-Shoah perspective
and all that this means. And we think together about these texts in the
context of theological questions.

There is a great deal of flexibility in our discussion even so.
The angles that can emerge in any of these three ways that shape our

---

[6] Eliezer Berkovitz, *With God in Hell* (New York: Sanhedrin Press, 1979),
pp. viii-ix.

dialogue already produce a potential for alternative readings. But this is our hope. I have argued elsewhere that all theology after the Shoah is midrashic.[7] That is to say, this theology explores a plurality of possible readings of our traditions, our texts, which may give possible meaning for us in connecting Sinai with Auschwitz. To set these alternative side by side, we create both an obvious ambiguity of meaning and a creative tension between readings (what Paul Ricoeur calls a conflict of interpretations[8]). This creative tension is a natural part of any open hermeneutical process, but it is especially vital for post-Shoah dialogue. We must be careful that we do not close off this creative tension, this ambiguity too early. The tension is in fact the driving force of new insight and ongoing conversation.

But our conversation is truly midrashic in that we aim not to accept mere ambiguity as if all meanings, all interpretations can hold equal validity for us in our making the connection between Auschwitz and Sinai. The process may, in fact, be more concerned not so much with finding a best reading of any text than with uncovering rules for reading that are now essential for our generation. Exciting new ideas might emerge, but a foundation that guides all of our reading, all of our conversation on any text or set of texts may be even more fruitful for our future. This open process is a primary aim for us and will, of course, lead us to reject some readings that cannot stand the crucible of the connection.

In a sense, then, the choice of specific text is arbitrary. If rules for reading apply for any text then we are likely to discover these guiding principles in dialogue on whatever texts we would choose. Surely, some texts are more central and more obviously important for the shaping of our unique religious identities. They are undoubtedly prime candidates for conversation. Yet, we should expect that basic principles forged by dialogue would produce the opportunity for ever new always developing discussion on new texts. Our choice here in this discussion, by that measure, is only a beginning. Our discussion is by nature open ended seeking to stay open to new possibilities and new texts.

As an illustration of this approach, I am looking at Deuteronomy 30:19-20. l like the idea of a short text even if the text is

---

[7] James F. Moore, *Christian Theology After the Shoah* (Lanham, MD:University Press of America, 1993), p. 21ff.
[8] Paul Ricoeur, *Le Conflit des Interpretations* (Paris: de Seuil, 1969).

clearly lifted from a larger context. I will try to account for this
context as I share with you the theological/dialogical reading of
biblical texts that I am proposing. First, let me set before us the text:

> The Text: "I call heaven and earth to witness against you today
> that I have set before you life and death, blessings and curses.
> Choose life so that you and your descendents may live, loving the
> Lord your God, obeying him, and holding fast to him; for that
> means life to you and length of days, so that you may life in the
> land that the Lord swore to give to your ancestors, to Abraham, to
> Isaac, and to Jacob." (NRSV)

Wiesel's Text:

> "Never shall I forget that night, the first night in camp,
> which has turned my life into one long night, seven times cursed
> and seven times sealed. Never shall I forget that smoke. Never
> shall I forget the little faces of children whose bodies I saw turned
> into wreaths of smoke beneath a silent blue sky.
> "Never shall I forget those flames which consumed my faith
> forever.
> "Never shall I forget the nocturnal silence which
> deprived me, for all eternity, of the desire to live. Never shall I
> forget those mountains which murdered my God and my soul and
> turned my dreams to dust. Never shall I forget these things, even
> if I am condemned to live as long as God Himself Never."[9]

My aim is to think with you only about the inter-play between the
Shoah and the text, that is the second form of inter-narrativity. When
this happens we have raised for us at least the following questions for
dialogue:
1.   The several pairs of both/and phrases in the text already
indicate the ambiguity for us (heaven and earth, life and death,
blessings and curses) with the sense that our choices are blurred even
when we appear to have choices. Note that I have not included the
other pair (you and your ancestors) because it is not set as an
ambiguous both/and but as an inclusive claim, that the choice is
effective for both the present generation and the future generations.
Still, that claim is now like the other pairs inverted in meaning in the
context of the Auschwitz narrative as indeed the choices of one

---

[9] Elie Wiesel, *NIGHT*, (New York: Bantam Books, 1960), p. 32

generation did set the fate of future generations. Thus, the issue of the text seems to be that of our choice and how we make choices. Set into the context of Auschwitz, the ambiguity of the choice that is resolved by the speaker in Deuteronomy (choose life) is inverted: a.) Either the choice presumed as life in the ancient text is converted by the context into a choice of death (to be obedient to the covenant means the choice of death or curse rather than the choice of life) or b) The choice is a non-choice and the elimination of choice and thus any basis for morality obliterates the message of Deuteronomy.

But, does this mean that the story of Auschwitz prevails and the story of the covenant is made mute in the face of the Nazi ideology which eliminated choice? If we read Wiesel's account of the first night in the camp, we are left with that sense (murdered my God forever). I intentionally set my comments in relation to Zev Garber's imagery in his Berlin essay in which he argues that when Auschwitz (survival at any price) contends with Sinai (a moral standard), Sinai must prevail. In fact in real terms, there is no necessity that assures that the moral standard will prevail.[10] Indeed, the reality is that Auschwitz prevailed and the point is that the loss of morality, especially in the notion that there is a standard that is worth dying for, that people will choose to hold fast in the face of such death, raises as many questions as it leads to answers.

And, the prevalence of the Auschwitz narrative eliminates the first ambiguity (heaven and earth) since the scene murders the God of the covenant (one who would bring blessing with the choice of a life of obedience).

2.   In the same way, the reading of Deuteronomy in the context of the Auschwitz narrative heightens the intensity of the ambiguity of life and death since this is not the natural interplay of the two that is part of all life but the imposed sentence of death that challenges moral sense completely. Even the notion that the choice of life meaning the choice of obedience, a picture drawn by Eliezer Berkovitz among many, is challenged by this inter-narrativity since it is not at all clear (a) that the choice of obedience is so unambiguously a choice of integrity which fights against the power of evil, in that survival at some cost may well be a better choice, or more to the point that the choice to steal life from death in real terms is potentially a more

---

[10] Zev Garber, *Shoah: The Paradigmatic Genocide* (Lanham, MD: University Press of America, 1994), p. 176.

integral choice, and (b) that the way that such texts emphasize, in such readings of them, the notion that it is better to die with integrity than to live, or that some values are worth dying for, challenges the very role that religion plays as a giver of meaning.

As a Christian thinker, I am especially troubled by this interplay of narratives since Christianity has as its central core narrative a narrative of a death, a choice to die, and the image of Jesus as the sacrifice which becomes normative moral behavior, which many read back into this notion of dying with religious integrity, is made even more problematic by this inter-narrative reading. This is especially true if we note further that Christianity at the very least is culpable for the narrative of Auschwitz, in that Christians were the perpetrators and Christianity was so easily manipulated as a justification. What then of this notion that there are values worth dying for?

The interplay between narratives leads right into the heart of a troubling aspect of religions that demand obedience in the face of death. This imagery of self-sacrifice even to death, the imagery so central to Christianity, so much a part of one way of thinking about Christian living, is called into question. This is even more the case when Christians can easily stretch the choice into a matter of eternal life thinking that the reward (blessing) to come is worth handing over life now. Such a view not only paves the way to religious extremism but now cannot really be upheld in the face of Wiesel's narrative about Auschwitz. Indeed, I am suggesting that a Christian reading of this text from Deuteronomy, if it is a post-Shoah reading, must take the focus on death out of the center and now read this text as a literal affirmation of life, present. life in all of its physicalness, all of its limitations, all of its humanity. I have argued before that one dictum that must characterize Christianity now is the obligation to safeguard Jewish life, lives. That grows out of a more primary focus that affirms life period and not death. And now we are left asking what does it mean to affirm a Christianity that no longer focuses on its central imagery of the cross but rather follows the appeal of Deuteronomy to choose life? Do we really have another choice post-Shoah? [Note: I am again reminded of Zev Garber's work, this time in an essay on deconstructing theodicy. In this essay, Zev argues that the danger of any religion and certainly for Christians and Jews is that fear of the evil one can become the central defining feature of the religious perspective. Surely, this fear is a potential consequence of Auschwitz but it is even more a potential consequence of radical moral religion in which the notion that we are right and there are those in every shadow that threaten us and our standards leads us directly into a religion defined by fear. What is worse is that such fear and actions built on it is justified in religions such as Christianity by an absolute authority giving absolute commands with ultimate choices. In another essay, Zev Garber argues that disputation within religion in which there is persistent paradox and no absolute understanding is finally our hope. I could not agree more.[11]]

---

[11] Ibid., Garber, p. 133, 168)

Chapter Two: Midrashic Christian Theology: Christian Theology for a Post-Shoah World

The paradoxical nature of the theme of this conference - remembering for the future - is surely felt most strongly in any effort to provide vision for theology for Judaism or Christianity. On the one hand, both Judaism and Christianity have built their respective thought traditions on remembering in order to understand how we should move forward. This is essentially the style of doing theology most clearly illustrated by Midrash. Thus, both Christians and Jews should be quite skilled at living and thinking within this paradox of remembering for the future. Still, the nature of the Shoah in our memories is so challenging that we hardly know how to remember to begin with let alone be bold enough that our remembering produces lessons that help us move forward. When our silences are broken, our silences that arise from the unbelievable events that took place still close enough to our generation that we can listen to eyewitnesses, we often find ourselves talking in simple statements like "never again." In fact, this kind of response seems the most appropriate, and to some the only, response possible. Instead of endless talk and reflection, we are thrust into acting, aiming our lives toward whatever signs and events that might signal the slightest return of the madness that motivated the Shoah. Thus, thinking about Christian theology at a time like this is both paradoxical and troubling.

Still, we know that thinking about theology is central to any new future that we can create. We are not trapped by the past as if we slavishly cling to that which is traditional out of habit, but the events of our respective traditions still are the shaping pieces of our identities, of our respective stories. It is through theology that we ask whether these stories, being either a Christian or a Jew, makes sense now and how we can live sensibly, morally as Christians or Jews in the future. It is through theology that we uncover both what is right and what is wrong about the tradition in order to ask the hard questions about how we must look differently at ourselves and others, at Christians and Jews now in order to fulfill our deepest desire to assure that never again will we face such madness or such apostasy as we found in the Nazi era, in our memories. Thus, even if thinking about Christian theology sets us face to face with paradoxes, with the core challenges that our memories bring us, we know that only by facing these challenges can we possibly move forward.

There is an urgency that propels us forward as well besides the urgency of never again. This urgency is the opportunity of the moment that we now face in dialogue. We now have the chance to find a radically new way for Christians to think about Jews, to talk about Jews, to relate to Jews. But the agenda for doing this, for taking hold of the opportunity is enormous in many ways. We dare not wait to take up the challenge, to sense the urgency of the situation, until we are more confident about the paradox. The time may fade more quickly than we imagine. Even now we face the dwindling number of those who were eyewitnesses.[1] Soon we will no longer have the personal check on our thinking that they represent. Even now we face those who are prepared to deny or at least re-write this history in order to justify ways of thinking that are not tolerable.[2] Even now there is a growing restlessness or even complacency that suggests that the thinking we find so necessary is not worth the effort. We dare not wait until we have greater confidence to speak. There is an urgency in the present opportunity.

How Shall We Move Forward

In fact, much has already been done to move us forward. Although still relatively few in number, there are leading theologians who have both spoken to the challenge of the Shoah for Christian theology and to the way that we move forward from these challenges. It is my intention in this paper to continue my exploration of these beginnings by searching what has been done by thinkers on key issues in Christian theology. In order to focus our thinking at this stage, I will narrow our conversation to the Pauline material as a primary source for the Christian theological

---

1. Any number of people have tried to gather taped interviews with survivors, the Yale project being the most expansive effort to preserve eyewitness accounts.

2. Cf., the very helpful book responding to this development:
    Franklin Littell, Irene Schur, and Claude Foster, ed. *In Answer...* (West Chester, Pa.: Sylvan Publishers, 1988).

traditions. Even though a thorough treatment of the impact of Pauline thought on Christianity is necessary in order to respond fully to the challenges of dialogue and the Shoah, this paper must serve only as a beginning taking up only select topics and a specific set of Pauline texts in order to make the task manageable. At any rate, this narrow set of concerns will surely serve us well as illustration of what must be done as well as what has already been done that we can build on.

Moving forward requires also clarifying the nature of our task as well as our subject. Thus, I turn first to identifying the nature of post-Shoah Christian theology, standing on the three pillars of dialogue, the challenge of the Shoah to Christian claims, and the demand for a new midrash. These foundations of post-Shoah Christian theology are, on the one hand, clearly evident in most post-Shoah Christian thinking. Still, there remains a range of perspectives that reflects not only a plurality of possible theologies but also the ambiguity in our work, especially in this time. This range of thinking shows both the broken nature of any theology when challenged by the Shoah as well as the potential to break new ground. By exploring this small segment of the work required in the way I propose, we can be led toward the threshold of new ground, of constructive proposals for Christian thought and life. That is, at least, the hope for this paper.

A Post-Shoah Christian Theology

Dialogue as Central

Several features of post-Shoah Christian theologies are assumed as beginning points. Of course, any such theology must take seriously the impact of the Shoah on all religious thinking. One way to do that is to work with a theology that has a memory, a theology that cannot be done without the memory of the six million (or as Irving Greenberg has argued, the more than one million children who died[3]). But, we may ask, how does a theology maintain a memory? Surely the extension of Greenberg's challenge, that no theology can be composed that could not be said in front of the one million children who died translates into a working foundation for any post-Shoah Christian theology. That foundation is that no Christian theology after the Shoah can be proposed that could not be said in the presence of our Jewish partners in dialogue.

---

3. Irving Greenberg, "Cloud of Smoke, Pillar of Fire," from *Auschwitz: Beginning of a New Era?*, Eva Fleischner, ed. (New York: KTAV, 1977).

Naturally, this foundation can developed in a full range of ways. Respect for the other does not imply mere agreement or even mere capitulation. On the other hand, certain theological positions do seem quite outside of what is acceptable in a post-Shoah Christian theology. We might suggest that a working rule of thumb is the kind of transformation suggested by Clark Williamson which moves us from a teaching of contempt toward a teaching of respect.[4] The basic features of what Jules Isaac called the teaching of contempt are clues about what is not now adequate as Christian theology.[5]

Still, even these fairly specific points are general in nature, not specific enough to pay attention to the subtle ways that a contempt can still be carried in theologies that are otherwise aimed at dialogue. Even more important are the ways that theology is done for the masses, that is, the way Christianity is taught and conveyed through the teaching and preaching and even the liturgy in churches. Thus, dialogue means speaking of Christianity in all settings as if our Jewish partners were present. We cannot relax this dictum even in familiar settings, even when we think we know our intentions. It is this far reaching diligence that is the meaning of dialogue as a foundation for post-Shoah Christian theology.

Plurality and Ambiguity as Ever Present Features of Theology
David Tracy has argued that all theological language after the Shoah is fraught with ambiguity.[6] In the context of the Shoah, even the most central and unshakable beliefs are shaken and transformed. We cannot say that forgiveness, or grace, or God's love, or hope for redemption can mean the same as they do outside of the context of the Shoah. To develop a theology with a memory, therefore, we must maintain this level of ambiguity. What we may have said with confidence before can now only be said with a level of uncertainty.

Nevertheless, this ambiguity does not make theology impossible.

---

4. Clark Williamson, *When Jews and Christians Meet* (St. Louis: CBP Press, 1989).

5. cf., my treatment of these themes in:

James Moore, *Christian Theology After the Shoah* (Lanham, Md.: University Press of America, 1993).

6. David Tracy, "Religious Values After the Holocaust: a Catholic View," in *Jews and Christians After the Holocaust*, Abraham Peck, ed. (Philadelphia: Fortress Press, 1982), p. 92ff.

At the very least, our theology is in its confidence (even if uncertain confidence) the most forceful response to the dark ideology of the Nazis. We must be able to retrieve our basic convictions in a way that maintains the memory. We do this by retrieving the plurality of possibilities within the tradition that allows for a theology that is open to the new challenges of each generation. This sense of openness, somewhat like the sense of oral Torah introduced by the rabbis, allows us to make the memory a part of our theology, a way to look for new applications and interpretations. All of this can be the way toward a post-Shoah theology so long as we maintain the memory, the negative hermeneutic in Tracy's language[7], that checks against interpretations that could not make sense to those who lived within the Shoah, not to mention those who survived and are still among us.

Moving Toward Midrash

The kind of retrieval I mention above is like a midrashic interpretation of Christian texts and tradition. What is done in such a theology will not be a copy of the ancient midrash of the rabbis but will be aimed at a similar result, the ongoing sense that our reading of scripture for the purpose of shaping theologies is to speak to this generation, the generation that stands on the far side of what Arthur Cohen called the tremendum.[8] This sort of theology is homiletical, then, with the aim not only of giving shape to academic theology but also to suggest ways for application in all settings where theology is done.

Of course, this means that our theologies will be heuristic in character, suggesting both a variety of possible directions for thought and application as well as rules for interpretation. We cannot presume that any theology will be final, absolute. Both the context of dialogue (now clearly evident in a community of people in dialogue) and the aim at preserving the ambiguity of any interpretation will mean that theologies are constantly open to new thinking and dialogue. Even as the events of the Shoah fade and the survivors are no longer with us, this theology can absorb the memories that have been taken up in theologies as resources for each new generation. We can set out on a massive journey approximating what Elizabeth Maxwell has said we need, a Christian Talmud.[9]

---

7. Ibid. Tracy.

8. Arthur A. Cohen, *The Tremendum* (New York: Crossroad, 1981).

9. She made this appeal in a lecture presented to the 22nd Annual Scholar's Conference on the Holocaust held in Seattle. Washington in March 1992. The

Bridging toward the Pauline Material

If our intent is to create the context of dialogue, then surely the Pauline material is at least as central for this task as any selection of Christian texts can be. The extended Pauline material has been centrally important for shaping Christian thinking through the ages. Much of the basic perception of the Jews passed on by succeeding generations of Christians has been built on the Pauline vision of Christianity and Judaism, at least as Christians have understood the Pauline material. Several key texts in the Pauline corpus are prime candidates for exploration especially in the way that they seem to justify, in the minds of many, some form of anti-Judaism, some form of the teaching of contempt.

Nevertheless, we need a way to set this material and, thus our discussion of it, into the context of the Shoah. We need to create a link in memory that makes our reflection on the Pauline material truly a post-Shoah theology. This bridge, very interestingly, might emerge from reflection on the post-Shoah Jewish discussion of the validity of the *mitzvoth* during and after the Shoah. This discussion so dramatically portrayed in the provocative thought of Eliezer Berkovits may very well give us the bridge we need since Berkovitz takes on those from within Jewish thought who denied that observance of the law and trusting the God of the covenant was of any value at all during the Shoah, even those who claim that such observance was not only valueless but even detrimental to Jewish survival.[10] Berkovitz' argument seems at one and the same time to reproduce the feel of the Pauline case in quite a different way and setting as well as call into question traditional ways of understanding Paul within Christian theology. That is, if Berkovits is right, then such an argument is an extremely direct challenge to stereotypical Pauline theology.

Eliezer Berkovits

Berkovits is not a bridge to Paul in a sympathetic way. It is not altogether clear that Berkovits welcomes constructive conversation with Christians at all. Judaism, for him, is quite sufficient in itself and would gain nothing at all from dialogue with Christians. This fact is all the more valuable for our purposes since Pauline thought has tended to be

proceedings are forthcoming from Edwin Mellen Press.
10. Eliezer Berkovitz, *With God in Hell* (New York: Sanhedrin Press, 1979).

interpreted as the exact opposite, that Judaism is incomplete and completely unable to bring salvation without the fulfillment of Jesus Christ. Whether this is an accurate reading of Paul's material, it is the typical view of Judaism that is attributed to Paul. Thus, Berkovits gives us as strong a case as we can imagine to counter this typical Pauline view.

Berkovits, of course, says nothing about the relation of his ideas with Christian claims. He is relatively unconcerned about that relationship, but is far more concerned with how other Jewish thinkers interpret the effectiveness of Judaism in the ghettoes and the camps. He seems especially concerned with views like those of Victor Frankl or Bruno Bettelheim.[11] The issue is whether observance of the commandments, that is orthodox Judaism, was an effective response to the Nazi challenge. Even more problematic is Bettelheim's claim that observance was, in fact, a serious threat to survival. Indeed, Elie Wiesel's account in *Night* seems to imply that Bettelheim was right, commitment to observance seriously limited the camp inmate and led to situations that threatened survival.[12]

It is this challenge that Berkovits sets out to refute. He does not wish to challenge either Frankl or Bettelheim in terms of the evidence that supports their case. The issue for Berkovits is not whether in some cases the observance did threaten physical survival. Berkovits would concede that, even spiritual lapse in such extreme circumstances was likely. His moving story of this effort to maintain a Jewish lifestyle told in *With God in Hell* is surely the best example of his effort to respond to Bettelheim and Frankl and make his case. As he says:

> "Though living through a persecution radically more severe than anything experienced previously, the Jews who suffered under the Nazis in essence continued the historic lifestyle of the Jewish people. To be sure, this lifestyle, as embodied in the *halakah*, is a style of living."[13]

This lifestyle is what Berkovits calls authentic selfhood and measures for him the whole of human existence, both physical and

---

11. see especially, Berkovitz, pp. 52ff.
12. I think especially of Wiesel's obligation to honor his father, an obligation that truly threatened his survival as accounted in:

    Elie Wiesel, *Night* (New York: Bantam Books, 1960).
13. Eliezer Berkovits, *With God in Hell*, p. 62.

spiritual, as worthy of concern. The issue for Berkovits is whether *halakah* was viable under the persecution of the Nazis. Even more, Berkovits believes that if the lifestyle could be shown to be viable even if for some it was not possible to maintain, then not only is the Jewish life preserved but it remains what is genuine, godly living. That notion is not only a challenge to Frankl and Bettelheim but also to any Christian who has accepted the typical view of Paul. Indeed, Irving Greenberg has argued that a major challenge to Christian thinking after the Shoah is the challenge to the Christian lifestyle as an authentic, genuine way of living.[14] The question becomes, 'Can we see, as Berkovits saw, an authentic Christian lifestyle that also endured the great persecution?' If we were to say yes to that question, how would we measure that life, by what or in what is that life embodied?

Let us concede for the moment that Berkovits has effectively made his point. Not only did Jewish living survive the Shoah and endure the Shoah but it did so without any assistance whatsoever from the culture, even from Christianity. No matter what we might claim about the rescuers (and they were a minority), it was not on account of heroic rescue by Christians or others that Judaism survived. As Berkovits argues, Jewish living survives because individuals and groups chose to make *halakah* the framework of their living. Those choices allowed for the flexible adaptation and adjustment that is, in fact, characteristic of "the law", within the extreme, extraordinary experience of the camps. Berkovits is correct in saying on these terms that Judaism is sufficient in itself quite apart from Christianity. Even more, the function of *halakah* in the camps stands as a complete counter testimony to the typically Pauline view of Judaism as bound to the law.

Of course, Berkovits must still respond to the critique of Wiesel asking how much suffering finally breaks the ability to trust.[15] When can

---

14. Greenberg, p. 12ff.
15. Actually, Wiesel has argued that he never speaks of God and the issue of whether trust or lack of it is critical is for Wiesel the same as for Berkovitz, an issue for those who were there at Auschwitz. This was his view at least in his famous exchange with Richard Rubenstein at the first Scholar's Conference on the Holocaust in Detroit (see, Franklin Littell and Hubert Locke, ed., *The German Church Struggle and the Holocaust*, Detroit: Wayne State Press, 1974). Still, we are reminded of the famous imagery from night that speaks volumes about broken trust (see, *Night*, p. 32).

we say that trust (*emunah*) in the God of the covenant is finally broken? This question remains a puzzle, and Berkovits cannot use the faithfulness of the people to a lifestyle as a justification for God even if he wanted to do so. For Berkovits, the genuineness of the lifestyle belongs in the faithful observance, in the application and not finally in some eschatological validation. Such a life would be valid, would be godly even if God fails God's promises entirely. Perhaps Berkovits would say this even, but the issue is not fully resolved and that doubt is not a doubt born from within the Shoah but after the Shoah. His point from the first is that those who would speak of faith or loss of faith after not having endured the great suffering really cannot speak about the genuineness of faith or doubt. Judgments like this are problematic after the fact.

All of this is a good bridge toward the Pauline material as the argument presented by Berkovits, principally to Frankl and Bettelheim, provides us with some important clues about how a new Pauline theology can be, must be a post-Shoah theology.

The Pauline Impact and Our Task

Since we cannot examine the whole Pauline corpus, we can judge the task ahead of us by identifying some of the Pauline influence on Christian theology. It is perhaps most common to think that Paul sets up a series of theological concepts (a good many dialectical pairs) that have shaped Christian theology as much as any of the early Christian writers. Thus, it is in the theology of Paul and not so much Paul's account of the story of Jesus that we look for Paul's impact and our task of retrieving the Pauline material for a post-Shoah Christian theology, and it is in these concepts and the dialectical pairs that we can best see Paul's theology -- e.g., law and gospel, sin and grace, flesh and spirit, faith and works. It is also clear that Paul's discussion of these concepts often leads to his characterizing the relationship between Christianity and what he calls the Jews and the Greeks.

What is not so often discussed is the manner of Paul's theology, although we face a similar question with Paul as we do with the teaching of Jesus. Is Paul, as he claims, a Pharisee with the training of Rabbinic teachers? Can we assume that he actually studied, as appears to be the claim, with Gamaliel? Ed Sanders treatment of Paul and Palestinian Judaism implies that there is little evidence to assume that Paul's Judaism corresponds with the Judaism of Palestine.[16] Fascinating and thorough as

16. E.P. Sanders, *Paul and Palestinian Judaism* (Philadelphia: Fortress Press,

Sanders is, his study does not fully disprove Paul's claim, only that Paul's view of Judaism seems to match more the state of Judaism in the diaspora. The question remains for us, is Paul fundamentally a Pharisee in his approach to themes, to theology? I believe that uncovering the Jewish character of Paul's theology is central to a possible retrieval of Paul's material.

Pauline Judaism and Theological Method
          Michael Cook argues that Paul's interpretation of the radiance of Moses is debateable and not self-evident.[17] That is, Paul's exegesis may be understandable given Paul's belief that the new dispensation had arrived in Christ Jesus, but it is only one of many possible interpretations, thus open to re-consideration. And, theological efforts to reject all other possible readings in favor of the Pauline view is only a later aberration in Christian theology brought about by the perception that Jewish obstinance had continued. Cook is quite right in saying that the reified and narrow reading of Pauline thought in later Christian theology is not appropriate for an age of dialogue. On the other hand, can we say with that Pauline material is irretrievable in our post-Shoah world. Certainly in this narrow reading we would say yes. On the other hand, if Paul's thought was intended as something quite different than it became, perhaps as a *midrash* or even as *halakah*, maybe we can think again about the role of the Pauline material in a post-Shoah Christian theology. It could be that the Pauline material is the best, maybe only, avenue into thinking about Jewish and Christian relations on the issue of a continuing *halakah*, on Christianity's relation to the rabbinic tradition of the Talmud.[18]
          There is considerable evidence to indicate that the Pauline corpus is written as a Christian halakic interpretation of Torah, which means that what may be significant about the Pauline material may be found especially in the transition to pragmatic application of theology to specific community

---

1977), pp. 543ff.
17. Michael Cook, "The Ties that Blind: An Exposition of II Corinthians 3:12-4:6 and Romans 11:7-10" in *When Jews and Christians Meet*, Jacob Petuchowski, ed., (Albany, NY: State University of New York Press, 1988), p. 125ff.
18. Peter Tomson argues that the task of *halakah* is central to Paul's purpose:
          Peter Tomson, *Paul and the Jewish Law* (Minneapolis: Fortress Press, 1990).

problems, that is in the shaping of Christian living and Christian lifestyle, and not in the abstracted and reified theology. If this is the case (and it is at least an option that provides a route toward a post-Shoah retrieval), then Pauline theology might be read quite differently than it has ordinarily been read and Paul's view of Judaism may be seen in quite a different light. That is, the Pauline texts should be read as a whole and not as parts divided as is often the case with the theological sections of the Pauline epistles. The questions that shape the community problem inform how the theology should be understood and not the other way around.

If this understanding of the Pauline corpus is a possible reading, then we must look at the whole of Paul's thinking as part of an ongoing process and not as a analytical argument as if he aims to settle the questions once and for all. Still, if we take this road of understanding Paul, we must deal with the troublesome claims that Jews find especially difficult. We must attempt to set Pauline texts into the context of dialogue (or if we are correct, to return the texts to the context of dialogue, which is their proper home). We can do this only partially with the aim of discovering rules for reading Paul by looking at specific texts and reflecting on how various thinkers have read Paul in a post-Shoah, dialogical climate. The texts can form the structure of our exploration and the thinkers can provide clues leading toward alternative readings.

A Spectrum of Interpretations

Any post-Shoah Christian reading of the Pauline material is bound to be complex. There is surely a full spectrum of ways that Pauline texts have been understood by Christians committed to a new dialogue with Jews. Already that spectrum of views (which we will reconstruct in part to assist our efforts) produces both ambiguity, some doubt about whether a single interpretation can be called the true reading, and plurality, an obviously rich set of alternative readings each of which may provide a basis for conversation. That complexity is enhanced by the plurality of ways that Christians have understood the impact of the Shoah and the history of Christian anti-Judaism on Christian theologizing. Since I have produced a sketch of that spectrum several times in earlier work, I will not reproduce a discussion of that spectrum except to place the thinking of those interpreters of Paul useful for our present discussion. Still, we see that besides the plurality and the ambiguity about our interpretations of Paul already coming from the dialogue, there are clear criteria for judging what is adequate for our theologies, criteria that have emerged from post-Shoah reflections on Christian anti-Judaism. While we may not be able to identify a single reading of Paul that is true we may discard some readings as unworkable post-Shoah Christian thinking. Some readings of Paul are surely more relatively adequate for our time than others and we can move toward preliminary judgments about the adequacy of these renderings.

We can begin to develop the plurality of views by looking at a text not often part of discussions in dialogue even though there are clearly obvious implications for dialogue in this text. I think of, for example, Romans 5:18-21:

> Romans 5: {18} Therefore just as one man's trespass led to condemnation for all, so one man's act of righteousness leads to justification and life for all. {19} For just as by the one man's disobedience the many were made sinners, so by the one man's obedience the many will be made righteous. {20} But law came in, with the result that the trespass multiplied; but where sin increased, grace abounded all the more,{21} so that, just as sin exercised dominion in death, so grace might also exercise dominion through justification leading to eternal life through Jesus Christ our Lord.

Before we measure how various different thinkers might interpret this text and its relevance for post-Shoah theology, we should set the context for what we have just quoted. One context is surely the entire Pauline corpus, most particularly Paul's thinking. On the one hand, this text above reflects rather well many of the central themes of Paul's theology, but we also must remember that some way must be introduced to give the wider necessary background to the meaning of several central terms. We can do that by working through the various commentators which will give us both a sense of plurality and ambiguity necessary for any post-Shoah theology.

The narrower context is the letter to the Romans, a work that has received enormous attention in Christian circles from earliest to more recent times. That is, we cannot begin to think about how to read even a short text unless we become aware of how the full Christian tradition has made Romans one of the central sources for Christian thinking. We need an hermeneutic of suspicion, to use Paul Ricoeur's notion, in order to free this text for fresh reading.[19] Then we can move ahead to think about how

19. Paul Ricoeur, *Freud and Philosophy: An Essay on Interpretation* (New Haven: Yale University Press, 1970), pp. 20-37.

25

to characterize the thrust of the full letter to the Romans. I have already suggested that we might be enlightened by reading Paul's intent in reverse order from what is normally done, by seeing that Paul intends to construct a *halakah*. Thus, the point may be best seen in the practical issues that are the occasion for the letter rather than the theological section which seems to be preamble. We move from the problem to the theology rather than the other way around.

The even narrower context is the section in which the text is embedded. It is difficult to separate pieces of the letter from the larger continuity of presentation, but there does seem to be a break after the completion of an argument at the end of chapter 3 at which point Paul moves to a discussion first of Abraham, then Adam and then our text which finishes chapter 5. We might also see that the next section (revealing perhaps of the practical context for the entire letter) moves to new topic but may help us get a sense of the point of Paul's journey through chapters 4 and 5. Thus, some sense of connection with the first part of chapter 6 will be helpful.

Managing all of this will be quite a challenge, but the resulting revelation about whether a retrieval of Pauline text in a post-Shoah world is possible or in what way it is feasible will surely be worth the struggle. Having established this preliminary reflection by using the short text above from Romans, we can, then, make some brief suggestions about how we might read other Pauline texts giving a couple of distinct examples.

Paul as the Prime Shaper of a New Religion

Several years ago Michael Cook argued that it was Paul and not Jesus who was the founder of Christianity for Judaism was the religion of Jesus but the religion of Paul was faith in Jesus as the Christ.[20] In fact, Cook shares this view with many who see that the writings of Paul mark a clear break from the piety of Judaism. Nothing more clearly displays this break than Paul's various comments on the Law. Precisely what Paul means by the Law is a matter of debate, but the many passages that are relevant to this discussion suggest that Judaism is associated with the Law, even the prime example, while Christ has done away with the demands of the Law. If this is Paul's view, then clearly we have a break from Jewish

---

20. cf., His allusion to this argument in:

Michael Cook, "Jesus and the Pharisees: The Problem as it Stands Today," *Journal of Ecumenical Studies*, Volume 15, number 3, Summer 1978, p. 444.

piety and the beginnings of a new religion.

    This general interpretation of Paul, in particular, Paul's relation to Judaism, is common among many interpreters either sympathetic to or ignorant of dialogue, but few are more clearly and more adamantly committed to this view than Rosemary Ruether, particularly in her *Faith and Fratricide*.[21] In fact, Ruether believes that both Paul and John move the split from Judaism a step further along by providing a clear expression of a theology of anti-Judaism. Paul, in Ruether's view, is theologically committed to oppose Judaism because Paul has raised a reified and ontologized Christology to the center of Christian belief. For Ruether, this focus on christology inevitably leads to anti-Judaism. Her well known conclusion is that anti-Judaism is the left hand of Christology.[22]

    There can be little doubt that Paul makes the Christ a central, even the central, tenet of Christian theology. This Christo-centrism can be seen, at least it seems, quite clearly in the short text we have chosen for illustration. Sin reigns in death but grace reigns through righteousness to eternal life through Jesus Christ. This entire section of Romans seems to be an argument for the centrality of Jesus as the Christ and the argument proceeds out of two narratives from Genesis -- the Abraham cycle and the story of the Garden of Eden. Even more, Paul makes of Adam and Abraham types that serve to clarify the radical distinction between those in Christ and those who are outside, even those who are part of the old covenant.

    Ruether argues that this section of Romans is clearly a Pauline effort to show that the gentile Christians are the true heirs of the covenant and the Jews have been rejected. Indeed, because the Christ is now central to the religion of Paul, Paul has no choice but to declare that Israel has lost its election. What is most significant for Ruether is that this theology, whether or not it is authentically Pauline, is the adopted view of early Christianity and has persisted in Christian thought since that time. That the Romans text implies that death and trespass are the result of the Law and life and righteousness come from the Christ, we would be hard pressed to conclude otherwise. The text implies that Jews who are blind to the revelation in Christ *are outside of God's grace.* Whatever Paul's

---

21. Rosemary Ruether, *Faith and Fratricide* (New York: Seabury Press, 1974).

22. cf., Ruether, *Faith and Fratricide*, p. 246.

sympathies are for Jews, his theology puts Jews outside of redemption. This notion of the blindness of the Jews that makes them the prime enemy of grace is, of course, one of the pillars of the teaching of contempt outlined by Jules Isaac. Ruether's claim is that this teaching flows inevitably from Paul's theology. That is, contempt for Judaism is bound to arise if this view is central to Christianity. The only way to erase this contempt from Christian thinking, according to Ruether, is to deny the authoritative status of this theology, of the ideas that emerge from Paul's reading of Judaism and of Christian belief. This approach to Paul, that of purging the text of its obvious flaws and underlying hatreds, is one approach to retrieving the texts. Whatever we might gain from Pauline material, from this view, must be re-thought from a radically new perspective that denies the validity of a Christo-centric view of scripture.

Ruether's radical approach may, in fact, be the only viable alternative to traditional Christian anti-Judaism. Anything short of radical surgery may well be futile. Still, the view seems to lose its workability for at least two reasons. First, the Pauline approach is so deeply imbedded in Christian thinking that such a radical denial of Pauline authority on such things would be practically impossible. It may work in conferences but it will be enormously difficult to apply in practice. Second, despite the undeniable historical evidence that Christian readings of Paul have led directly to anti-Judaism, a teaching of contempt and even open antisemitism, it is not self-evident that Paul's Christo-centrism does in fact require anti-Judaism. Ruether's reading of Paul, as persuasive as it is, is not the only reading of Paul, and a different approach may indicate a more practically workable theology.

Paul As Reformer of Judaism

Actually, scholars who hold that Paul was a Jewish reformer, that Paul essentially viewed himself as extending and revising the work of Judaism, move in two quite different directions. Some hold that Paul saw his work as fundamentally a revision of his own belief and life and that his theology reflects his response to his own Judaism and to Jews. Lloyd Gaston reflects this view to an extent as he holds that Paul's work is Judaism extended by a belief in the centrality of the Christ event.[23] Darrell Fasching thinks along similar lines although he views Paul's reform as a message to the Gentiles, a theology that allows for the holding of two

---

23. cf., Lloyd Gaston, *Paul and the Torah* (Vancouver: University of British Columbia Press, 1987), p. 5ff.

contradictory themes -- that the whole of Israel will be redeemed and that Israel was for the moment enemies for the sake of God's work among the Gentiles.[24] As an internal view of Paul's thinking and theology both of these views may be defended quite adequately.

The first notion of reform, a view of the reform of Judaism by the Christ principle, would mean that, for example, Paul in *Romans* means his discussion of the two Adams as a discussion of universal history which includes the role of the Jewish people. Death comes not from the law but from sin, the sin of the first Adam. The law is a second episode in this history in which knowledge of God's righteousness shows all the more clearly the effect of sin, not merely death but the sin-infected life. For those like Gaston, then, the law comes as a part of God's grace, a part of the plan of God for redemption. Law is not, thereby, nullified by Christ but the plan of God's salvation is expanded to bring the possibility of eternal life in Christ.

The full meaning of this theology is still in need of development, but in a brief way, this thinking makes the role of the Jewish people a series of stages now moved into a more universal stage by the event of the Christ. The talk of freedom from the law is not, then, an abrogation of the law but talk of the change (or renewal) of focus. Just as God led the people from Egypt for the sake of redeeming the world, God now leads the Jewish people back into the world for the same purpose. The implication is something like the view of Emil Fackenheim as he calls Israel back to a mission to mend the world.[25]

Fasching's view is similar in that Paul intends to reform his own Judaism but his message is not so much for Jews but for Gentiles as Paul continues to hold himself faithful to a strictly Gentile mission. But the intent is to introduce gentiles to the true Judaism, the completed Judaism that depends fully on God's redemption and has nothing to do with human activity at all. If gentiles are to participate in God's redemptive activity, they cannot do so by making grace into a human achievement. They, too, must move through the stages of redemption as have the Jews. They must be confronted by the law that shows both the abundance of sin in human living (so that we can see clearly God's righteousness) and the super-

---

24. Darrell Fasching, *Narrative Theology After Auschwitz* (Minneapolis: Fortress Press, 1991), p. 33.

25. I refer to Fackenheim's developing thesis that comes to full expression in:

Emil Fackenheim, *To Mend the World* (New York: Schocken Books, 1982).

abundance of God's grace.[26]

  Now, there may be many versions of these views and my brief description of Gaston and Fasching does not do justice to the complexity of their thinking. But if I have captured the spirit of their thought, then we can see readily the issues that remain for dialogue. Even if Paul remains connected to his Judaism in some way seeking to reform that Judaism through the Christ principle, the followers of Paul make from Paul a new religion. The issue is still what constitutes reform and whether Paul's solution, even accepting his radical Christ-centered approach, was correct given the history of its effect. Does the sincere spirit of reform no matter how well grounded ultimately produce resentment when the reforms are not heeded or the connections are finally broken. Given Paul's theology, the matter is left to God's grace, but the impact of that theology may well have been a teaching of contempt and a legacy of murderous hatred. Gaston is surely aware of this issue as is Fasching. To understand Paul as reformer does not produce a workable theology for a post-Shoah world nor does it readily produce a way to retrieve Paul's thought for a post-Shoah theology.

  We may gain much if qualifiers are added to the way Paul is used in preaching and teaching in churches. At least we can eliminate some of the overt teaching of contempt that sneaks into our present theologies and preaching. But to put Paul in his place does not create bridges for retrieval. We are left only with traditional ways of applying Paul to Christian theology, albeit now qualified. Perhaps Ruether's view is more immediately effective, unless such a view of Paul as reformer is matched with a way of linking with the Shoah, with how theology must be in a specifically post-Shoah world. Fasching clearly has made that effort and we will attempt to bring such a post-Shoah view into play in this paper.

  Still, this view does lead us to the brink of yet another problematic in this effort to construct a post-Shoah theology. The salvation history thematic that is associated with both the view of Gaston and that of Fasching is, itself, challenged by the Shoah. That where sin abounds grace abounds even more, in Paul's words, is precisely the issue that the Shoah makes central (whether the theology is either Jewish or Christian). At the very least, trust in such redemption is claimed only in the face of incredible evidence to the contrary. This is, in fact, the issue that we brought into our

---

26. Fasching, pp. 34ff.

discussion with our treatment of Berkovits. If God is to be trusted or if Judaism is viable (not to mention Christianity) is precisely the issue even if it is a reformed Judaism in the form of Fackenheim's or Paul's call.

The Two Covenant Approach

Our use of the short text from Romans is already bearing fruit in this survey. At least, we can see with some clarity whether such texts can be retrieved effectively for post-Shoah Christian theology. This clarity is also evident when thinking about Paul's thought as a radical two covenant approach. I have argued that Paul van Buren's thought is most representative of this line of thinking.[27] In fact, van Buren has written so much on the subject that his thought would be extremely difficult to label by such rigid categories, and he has explicitly argued that his is not a theology of two covenants. Still, I think his position requires a two covenant approach and if that is lost some of his most significant contribution to the dialogue will also be missed.[28]

Van Buren argues that Jesus (the historical Jesus) is the link between gentile Christianity and Judaism. Thus, Christians worship through belief in Jesus the God of Israel and must continue to think of Jews as the Israel of God. This historical connection must not be lost if Christianity is to reclaim its validity and anti-Judaism is to be erased from Christian thought. That Jesus is the link is a curious but rather standard way of thinking. On the other hand, van Buren hopes for a view that escapes the traditional supercessionism that is associated with the standard view of Jesus. Thus, Jesus does not replace Judaism or the covenant with the Jewish people. Instead, somewhat like the views of Paul as reformer, van Buren sees Jesus as the occasion for expanding the covenant with Israel to the gentiles. In essence, Christianity becomes Judaism for the gentiles.[29]

---

27. cf., James F. Moore, "A Spectrum of Views: Traditional Christian Responses to the Holocaust," *Journal of Ecumenical Studies*, 25:2, Spring 1988, pp. 212-224.
28. This claim may be especially true of Van Buren's first volume of his trilogy - A Theology of the Jewish-Christian Reality - which is strongly refuted (even though his position does not seem to shift dramatically) in the last volume. See:

Paul Van Buren, *Theology of the Jewish-Christian Reality* (San Francisco: Harper and Row, 1980, 1983, 1988).
29. This way of putting Van Buren's argument is too simplistic as the

This view, despite van Buren's protests results in a two covenant position. If the covenant with Israel is to be maintained intact, then Christianity cannot be Judaism in any form. The rather loose phrase, "Judaism for the Gentiles" must mean that some other arrangement allows for Christianity to bring the promises and hopes of Israel to the nations. There must be two distinct redemptive agreements, even if the covenant with Israel already foresees the mission to the gentiles. The character of this covenant with the gentiles is both the promise of God's grace and a way of life. The task of Christians, like that of Jews, is to discern the way of the God of Israel.

Now this position is also like a traditional view, that of Rabbinic Judaism. Both aspects of what van Buren associates with Christianity are already present in Rabbinic views of the gentiles. On the one hand, the rabbis already were developing a way to think of God's relation with the gentiles, the so-called Noachide laws.[30] That is, rabbinic Judaism has traditionally allowed for a two covenant position. Likewise, Rabbinic Judaism saw that the covenant essentially includes God's promise and the commitment to discern the way of the God of Israel. That process of discernment was brought under the heading of "Oral Torah" and has been preserved in the traditions and materials of Midrash and in the great work of the rabbis in the Talmud in providing both *aggadah* and *halakah*. Thus, Christianity provides nothing of anything unique, the mission to and acceptance of the gentiles is already in place.

Any such position as that of van Buren faces this problem. Why should Christianity emerge as a separate movement when Judaism already possessed the exact means for engaging in a mission to the nations? Van Buren argues that the occasion of the historical Jesus is the catalyst for the new movement, an historical event that was so momentous that this new movement among the gentiles arose, in fact, grew into something quite different than that which was projected by Rabbinic Judaism. This

---

invitation to gentiles to participate in the way of God is, for Van Buren, something new, but it is not so new as to mean a different way than the way given to Israel. Thus, this is Judaism for gentiles in that sense.

cf. Van Buren, *Discerning the Way: A Theology of the Jewish-Christian Reality* - Vol. 1, pp. 138ff.

30. cf., the discussions in:

Lloyd Gaston, *Paul and the Torah*, pp. 23ff., and

Alan Segal, *Paul the Convert* (New Haven: Yale University Press, 1990), pp. 187ff.

momentous event, for van Buren, centers on the experience of the
resurrection in the new Christian community.[31] That is, no matter what
might have happened historically, the church bore witness to the
experience of the risen Christ that made the new movement necessary.

Of course, van Buren's position is complex and in need of more
attention than we can give him in this essay, attention that others have
attended to well. The presence of the two covenants is much more an
ontological and not essentially an historical event. The movement depends
on the experience of the Christ and not so much on the details of the
historical resurrection. We have argued elsewhere that this ontological
necessity makes van Buren's view susceptible to an ahistoricalness (there is
little to distinguish between the experience of the Christ in Paul from my
experience).[32] This lack of historicality becomes quite significant when we
address the issues emerging from the Shoah. Still, we can see that in this
view, Paul becomes the prototype of every Christian. The apostle is unique
in his connection to the Israel of God (he does not need Jesus to provide the
link to Judaism), but his relation to the new movement is precisely one
built on the experience of the Christ rather than the knowledge of the
historical details of Jesus.

It follows that Paul's thinking is a fundamental groundwork for
shaping what would become the key themes of the new Christ movement.
This role for Paul can be seen in applying the notions of van Buren to the
text we have been exploring from Romans. Paul's response to the Christ

---

31. It is this argument that suggests the necessity for a two-covenant view
rather than the more ambiguous single covenant notion that Van Buren often
believes he is offering. The resurrection of Jesus is for Van Buren a strikingly
new event that moves beyond what was present in the Mosaic covenant even
as it does not cancel or replace that earlier covenant. Cf., *Discerning the Way*,
pp. 190ff.

32. My original argument can be found in:

James F. Moore, "The Holocaust and Christian Theology: A
Spectrum of Views on the Crucifixion and the Resurrection in Light of the
Holocaust" in *Remembering for the Future*, Volume 1 (Oxford: Pergamon
Press, 1989), pp. 844-857.

Also, this view is supported in:

A. Roy Eckardt, *Reclaiming the Jesus of History* (Minneapolis:
Fortress Press, 1992), p. 175.

has led him to recast his view of history in order to place history in larger plan (not subject to the events of history but to the aims of God using history). In this view the law plays a two-fold purpose. On the one hand, the law remains the foundation of the covenant with Israel which serves to bring both knowledge of sin and the abundance of grace. In this view, Paul does not reject or alter the meaning of Torah and *halakah* for Israel. However, in addition to the power of the law for Israel, now righteousness has also become possible for the gentiles through Jesus Christ. This is not all we can say of this view. Van Buren does lead us to see that linking Christianity to its Jewish roots helps us to see that Christianity is also involved in discerning the way. That is, Paul is also a prototype for Christian *halakah*, his thinking aimed at making explicit the way of life now made possible for gentiles through the Christ. The two-pronged themes of sin and grace present already in the giving of the Torah are now translated into a way of living for the gentiles, a Christian *halakah*. It is, however, the case that Christian thinking has seldom viewed the life of Christian discipleship as *halakah* in the vein of rabbinic thinking. Paul has more often been read so that grace and law are made polar opposites and the task of *halakah* the great villainy of Pharisaic Judaism. At least van Buren has broken the back of the atrocious view that grace and law are enemies.

If Paul is a source for Christian *halakah*, then we truly have returned to Berkovits' dilemma. Christian living faces a similar challenge as Jewish living given the horrors of the Shoah. Can Christians defend the sense of a Christian way of life after what has taken place. In one significant way, Christians have an even greater dilemma; to act as Christians may have been a source for hiding under the Nazi onslaught at least in some ways. To recover Christian *halakah* is to challenge what has been seen as traditional Christian living. It is, in a sense, to begin again, to re-construct.

Paul the Pharisee, a Reconstruction of Christian *Halakah*

In fact, van Buren's position makes the matter of Christian lifestyle all the more problematic. On the one hand, discerning the way has been re-connected with the Jewish roots, but much like the problem of orthodox *halakah* that we encounter in Berkovits, the status of Christian lifestyle is not dependent on history. Genuine Christian living is rooted in the unalterable status of torah and of the oral torah (Jesus?).[33] Thus, the

---

33. This claim really functions as an implication of the fundamental

events of history do not change the details of *halakah*, only the questions. Of course, the beauty of the rabbinic system is that its midrashic style allows for the encounter with new questions and thus the ever expanding applicability of the torah to life situations. In that sense, midrash and Talmud are always existential but they are rooted in the undisturbed nature of written torah. Van Buren's view will always suffer this as well; there can never truly be a post-Shoah Christian theology that was not also genuine as pre-Shoah Christian theology.

This is the paradox of the tradition that van Buren links Christianity to. On the other hand, Berkovits really aims to break this problem precisely because he wants to take both Frankl and Bettelheim seriously in order to counteract their claims. The issue is precisely whether Judaism in its orthodox form is still viable in the historical crucible of the Shoah. Even if Berkovits senses the difficulty of making that argument very much like Irving Greenberg senses that difficulty, his approach aims at a retrieval in history built on the utter confidence that *halakah* can be retrieved.[34] We need to take van Buren that step further as well, to attempt a retrieval within history rather than in spite of history.

Such a retrieval requires taking the actual experiences of the Shoah as historically unique. The experience of both evil and God in the Shoah is not the same as Paul's experience of the Christ. We cannot assume that the Christian lifestyle is unaffected by this watershed of history. If we do take the Shoah seriously as a unique event in our religious history, then our reading of Paul will be more than the extraordinarily insightful two covenant approach of van Buren. We need to see Paul in the light of a theology that already embraces the ambiguity and openendedness that David Tracy and Johannes Metz have argued must be integral to any post-Shoah Christian theology.[35] To do this, we must set Pauline thought back into its historical context as Fackenheim has argued that Jews must return to history.

---

understanding of revelation that is characteristic of the way, that revelation is an accepted interpretation of the tradition and that the content of revelation is the reality of God (Van Buren, p. 37ff.). Thus we have both torah and oral Torah.

34. cf., Berkovits, *With God in Hell*, pp. 154ff.

35. see Tracy, "Religious Views After the Holocaust," p. 92, and
        Johannes Baptist Metz, *The Emergent Church* (New York: Crossroad, 1981), p. 28.

That context is the formative stages of a conversation about the nature of Jewish life. In this view, Paul remains what he claims to be, a Pharisee. Of course, two features of Paul's thought, at least, make that view of Paul difficult. First, Paul argues for the inclusion of gentiles into the community of believers. His view is of a single covenant that involves both gentiles and Jews. This creates a deep paradox that is not resolved by Paul in his writings but remains a question, troubling as it is, lurking in the midst of his various efforts to speak to practical issues of the early church. The only way to maintain the force of the paradox in creative tension is to create a view that holds the factions in ongoing dialogue, the contrasting, possibly contradictory, views in creative tension. The issue is whether there can be a *halakah* for gentiles that makes a unified community possible. That is by no means clear in Paul. Thus, Paul could be read as one offering a new way of thinking about Torah that remains an open question. His confidence may lead us unfortunately to assume prematurely that the issue is settled for Paul. Such is the character of this writer and thinker.

The second problematic is Paul's assertion of the centrality of the Christ. All this would be troublesome in the same way that we are troubled by van Buren's ahistoricalness if Paul's claim were perceived as an ontological claim and not as a means for thinking about *halakah*. If the Christ and the resurrection were seen as a proleptic event (as is enticingly hinted at by Rosemary Ruether or is more clearly presented by Roy Eckardt)[36], then the notion that a new religion is born in this event or that the Christ produces an historical event that changes our reality is made more problematic. Instead, the Christ event is a focussing event in which a lifestyle particularly in relation to the question of a gentile *halakah* is made clearer. Again we have a paradox in which some believers see insight in the life and death of Jesus and some do not see that at all. What emerges are two visions of the meaning of Torah, two missions in the world to mend the world. The issue about which is more valid is not yet resolved. Indeed, as Darrell Fasching argues, Paul's intent is to leave the resolution in the hands of God. It is perfectly possible that in the interim both missions have a unique validity.[37]

---

36. Ruether, *Faith and Fratricide*, p. 246ff., and

A. Roy Eckardt and Alice Eckardt, *Long Night's Journey Into Day* (Detroit: Wayne State University Press, 1982), p. 150.

37. Fasching, p. 33ff.

But of course, the challenge of the Shoah made clear in both the work of Irving Greenberg and Eliezer Berkovits is a challenge to the validity of both of these potential visions and missions. Neither can move forward without having a touchstone in history and the particulars of whether there can be a gentile *halakah* and what that might be have change in post-Shoah Christian theology. As with Jewish thinking, not only the questions but the content of the *halakah* have changed because of what has happened. This is the position held as the most appropriate avenue forward in this paper and will become the basis for reading the texts of Paul for a post-Shoah Christian theology presented in this paper. I realize that each of the other possible positions have much to suggest for such a theology and to dismiss them would not benefit us, but this final position does help us see something new in this discussion and can be made to incorporate the best of the other views we have discussed.

A Gentile *Halakah*??

We have the same difficulty in speaking of a gentile *halakah* as we do of a Christian *midrash*. In fact, the problem is even greater since it is precisely the *halakah* that has been the distinguishing feature of Judaism as compared with the development of Christianity. It is also this issue that has often been seen as the foundation for Paul's influence in shaping a new religion. Since the *halakah* is rooted in the Torah and gentiles have no need to live out of the Torah unless they are converted, the phrase "gentile *halakah*" is apparently a contradiction of terms. And we must avoid the implication of supercessionism that has plagued Christianity's treatment of the *halakah* and the assumption that the gentiles are the true heirs of the promise. We do not seek to understand the possibility of a gentile *halakah* so as to set up a competition between rabbinic Judaism and Pauline Christianity. That result would be the exact opposite of our intent.

Why, then, do we need to think of Paul's thought in terms of a gentile *halakah*? Our reason is that any other way of treating Pauline material has the potential to lapse into a teaching of contempt. We cannot fully demonstrate that claim in this paper, but we can produce the foundation for a fresh reading of Paul for theology that does take seriously our three pronged approach to post-Shoah Christian theology: (1) that any Christian theology must now be a theology in dialogue, (2) that any Christian theology must now be responsive to the challenge of the Shoah, and (3) any Christian theology must now be revised by returning to the roots of our thinking (a radical theology). We can do that especially well if we think of Pauline thought already as *halakah* thus enabling us to ask whether there is a valid post-Shoah Christian *halakah*.

As we have suggested, this approach to Paul requires that Christian theology think of Paul in the reverse fashion from what is traditional. Traditionally, Christians have thought of Paul's theology as basic; thus Paul's advice to the churches is seen as an outgrowth of Paul Christ-centered theology. In fact, a number of the thinkers we have alluded to by our spectrum of positions above continue to think of Pauline thought in this way. If we reverse that pattern, then we must assume that Paul's theology (the Christ-centered approach) is an outgrowth of his effort to produce a gentile *halakah*. In order to understand Paul's theology, therefore, we must uncover both what the practical question is in his letters and precisely what portion of Torah has become the resource for addressing the practical, lifestyle issue being considered. Only with this information clarified can we, then, make sense of the theology of Paul and thus make use of the various approaches to post-Shoah Pauline thought we have discussed thus far.

We can illustrate this approach only by turning to the texts of Paul (only a few examples can be offered here) in order to follow this pattern of treatment. We can begin by completing our treatment of the short text from Romans that has been our focus through this section of the paper. We recall that Paul writes in Romans that sin came into the world through one human (Adam) which leads to the condemnation of all humanity which has been reversed by the righteousness of one human (Jesus Christ). In addition, Paul argues that the law was introduced in order to increase the sin (more that we know of sin through the revealing of Torah), but that at the same time God's grace increases all the more. This passage from Romans 5 is representative of the heart of Pauline theology. We ask, how does this new approach we suggest allow for a fresh view of Romans 5 and the core of Pauline theology?

We can judge the impact of an halakic approach only by locating the issue at stake for Paul. We may find that offering a possible example is too limiting; that any true post-Shoah interpretation of Paul must be more thorough. Of course, this objection is correct. We offer only one possible approach in order to illustrate the fruits of this approach. The structure of the epistle to the Romans makes the turn to Romans 12 crucial. It is with Romans 12:1 that Paul appears to launch a description of a possible gentile *halakah* together with key issues that demand such an approach. That text begins with a central description of the problem at the center of Paul's concern:

> {12:1} I appeal to you therefore, brothers and sisters, by the mercies of God, to present your bodies as a living sacrifice, holy and acceptable to God, which is your spiritual worship. {2} Do not be conformed to this world, but be transformed by the renewing of your minds, so that you may discern what is the will of God–what is good and acceptable and perfect.

At the heart of gentile living that is shaped by the Torah is the issue of conforming to the world. This central Pauline theme is not to be taken as an invitation to exit the challenges of living in the world but rather as a question of whether living as Christians in the world is possible without conforming to the world. At least, within the Roman world, such a challenge was real since gentiles are not born as children of Israel but as citizens of the Roman state (we use the word citizen here somewhat loosely). The temptation to conform to the culture is even more powerful for the gentile precisely because they do not have a *halakah* that specifically identifies a path for living out of Torah. What is needed is a transformation that can happen only by introducing another way, a Christian lifestyle that can be adopted by gentiles who have been turned to the way.

It is significant that this passage from Romans 12 follows immediately upon Paul's discussion of Jewish-Christian relations in Chapters 9-11. On the one hand, we must assume that seeing the issue of Romans 12 as the key for understanding Paul must give insight into how one should read Romans 11, a point for consideration below. On the other hand, Paul's reference to the mercies of God seems especially tied to the discussion that immediately precedes this appeal to churches in Rome. The mercies of God are twofold in Romans 11, coming to the gentiles through Jesus Christ and to the Jews through the promise to the fathers. That is, Paul may very well have recognized the need for two different lifestyles - Jewish and Gentile, at least in the interim period in which he was living. Both have validity and both may well be included in Paul's treatment of the more specific issues that follow in Romans.

Indeed, because this is likely, the text begs for dialogue on this discourse by Paul. The opening of the passage which speaks of what is holy and acceptable is an implicit reference to the holiness code and the notion of presenting ourselves as a living sacrifice adds to this apparent larger context for Paul's thinking. The foundation for Christian living is the holiness code even if this for gentiles takes place through the person of Jesus the Christ. The issue becomes whether Paul is faithful to that implication and whether his desire to construct an *halakah* for gentiles in the fashion of Rabbinic thought actually works. No post-Shoah Christian retrieval of Paul's effort can possibly be valid outside of such a dialogue (even if that dialogue includes skepticism from Jewish dialogue partners about the whole project).

Even so, this text which identifies conforming to the world as the key issue for a gentile Christian lifestyle does enlightens us about how we ought to read a theological text like the one from Romans 5 that we have already seen in the light of various different Christian views of Paul. If we are correct, then Paul's reading of the Genesis texts concerning Adam are to be set into the practical context of the struggle to conform to this world. In the struggle to be transformed by a renewal of our minds, Adam does become the model of the one who is persuaded by his circumstances as opposed to the will of God (let us avoid the sexist implication that Adam fell prey to the temptations of Eve). In fact, the whole narrative from Genesis 2 and 3 suggests this conflict between the commands of God and the temptations of the human spirit to be central for understanding our general situation. Adam is a key example of the very issue which so concerns Paul in his letter to the Roman churches, that of conforming to the culture.[38]

If this reading fits, then Paul's twofold reading of history in Romans 5 suggests that he has already accepted the theological foundation for developing a *halakah* that enables the follower to battle against the urge to conform as including two episodes. First, the law is given which both shows the effects of sin (of conforming to the world in opposition to the will of God) and the abundance of God's grace (the possibilities of being transformed). For the gentiles, however, Jesus Christ, the one who is righteous, becomes the sign both of the effect of sin and the possibility for renewed living. That is, Jesus is for Christians what we have said elsewhere, the oral torah. The implication of Romans 5 is that in this new

---

38. This correspondence between Paul's thought and Genesis is surely picked up by:

     Francis Watson, *Paul, Judaism and the Gentiles* (Cambridge: Cambridge University Press, 1986), pp. 151-153.

age both Jews who follow teaching of Torah through the rabbis and gentiles who have been brought to the Torah through Jesus share a mission, the mission of being transformed and, thus, resisting the urge to conform to the world in opposition to the will of God. Indeed, Paul's language in Romans 12 -- "that you may discern (prove) what is the will of God" -- already implies that the challenge is more than mere individualistic transformation but also a mission to the world.

This has to mean that in God's plan the rabbinic *halakah*, which is at the time of Paul only beginning to take shape, and Paul's notion of a gentile *halakah*, which is the heart and soul of Paul's thought, ought to work in tandem for the sake of God's overall intention to redeem the world. Since Paul stood in history at a time when neither a developed Talmud nor a complete gentile Christian ethic had been shaped, he could only see this mission in eschatological terms, as something that would be finished in God's good time in the future. That this shared but separate participation in mission to the world seems at least to be a possible reading of Paul allows us to think of retrieving the Pauline texts in a different fashion, at least. The issue that remains is whether Paul's vision of shared mission effectively survives the challenge of the Shoah. Indeed, this is the question that Eliezer Berkovits poses for us. Is it enough to preserve a *halakah* (if we can even think of a gentile lifestyle) if the Christian *halakah* does not issue in behavior that reflects that lifestyle? The Shoah is precisely the challenging circumstance in which the Pauline call can be tested, that Christians might "prove what is good and acceptable and perfect" or whether Christianity has succumbed as Paul feared to conforming to the world. Isn't this the key question for us post-Shoah? And how can we respond if we have no sense of what a Christian *halakah* might be? At least, now post-Shoah we have reason to retrieve Paul's thought in the effort to construct a Christian *halakah* which allows to make a judgment about the shape of Christianity within the Shoah as well as the shape of a legitimate post-Shoah Christian ethic.

Some Examples of Retrieval

Peter Tomson has explored the idea of taking the Pauline material as *halakah* as seriously as anyone, I believe, but his work is indicative of the problem that we face in carrying forward a truly post-Shoah retrieval of Paul.[39] The halakic passages in Paul are quite important

---

39. That is, he does not integrate the Shoah factor into his reading and retrieval of Pauline *halakah*:

for Tomson but he still views these encounters with practical issues as journeys into incidental material. Thus, Tomson can separate Romans 14-15 from the rest of the letter as something quite different from the theological exposè of the earlier chapters. We cannot presume that Paul aims at *halakah* and at the same time treat the practical issues that give context for this as detours along the way. We are looking to reverse the normal pattern of interpretation. Romans 14-15 are central for understanding the theological development of the earlier chapters. Without the practical issues we would not have the theology.

This means that we must re-think the theology of Romans seeing the development of Paul's position theologically as a necessary implication of his intent to form a gentile *halakah* that allows for a community in which both Jewish lifestyle and Christian lifestyle are joined in a partnership in mission. We begin with the practical matters, such as can be found in Romans 14 in order to locate the meaning of the theology (say of Romans 2:25-29 or of Romans 4:9-12 not to mention Romans 9-11.) This means as well that the halakah that evolves from Paul's effort to address the practical issues must allow for a mutual respect between Jews and Gentiles. Any way of living that would serve to breed contempt is unthinkable for Paul, and such is quite evident in Romans 14. Our contemporary criterion is similar, that all Christian theology should serve to honor Jewish thought and life and no post-Shoah Christian theology is valid outside of this dialogue of mutual respect. I have already suggested the potential for dialogue on one matter and we can extend this heuristic exercise by noting other opportunities for dialogue aimed at testing the validity of a post-Shoah Christian *halakah*.

Work such as that of Tomson may be quite useful for us nevertheless as we test possible interpretations, but we must also say that we aim at a post-Shoah Christian theology. While our efforts will show that a plurality of interpretations of Paul are possible, only certain readings can survive the test of the Shoah. For example, Paul's concern for resisting our urge to conform to the culture around can be an enticing post-Shoah Christian theme, but Paul's halakic suggestions lead us in multiple directions extending from indifference to the wider culture to open collaboration with secular authorities, to open resistance. Paul's halakic model, as adequate as it might have been for first century Christianity might prove inadequate for post-Shoah Christianity. But that is the

---

Tomson, *Paul and the Jewish Law*, 1990.

question we have set before ourselves from the outset, especially with our description of Berkovits' argument.

Thus, a retrieval of Pauline material might begin with this fresh approach to Paul (moving from the practical issues to the theology), but must also satisfy the dual criteria of dialogue and the post-Shoah challenge to all Christian theology. Thinking about Romans 14 may help us see precisely how this three pronged treatment of Paul works. I set the text before us in order to help our conversation.

{14:1} Welcome those who are weak in faith, but not for the purpose of quarreling over opinions. {2} Some believe in eating anything, while the weak eat only vegetables. {3} Those who eat must not despise those who abstain, and those who abstain must not pass judgment on those who eat; for God has welcomed them. {4} Who are you to pass judgment on servants of another? It is before their own lord that they stand or fall. And they will be upheld, for the Lord is able to make them stand. {5} Some judge one day to be better than another, while others judge all days to be alike. Let all be fully convinced in their own minds. {6} Those who observe the day, observe it in honor of the Lord. Also those who eat, eat in honor of the Lord, since they give thanks to God; while those who abstain, abstain in honor of the Lord and give thanks to God. {7} We do not live to ourselves, and we do not die to ourselves. {8} If we live, we live to the Lord, and if we die, we die to the Lord; so then, whether we live or whether we die, we are the Lord's. {9} For to this end Christ died and lived again, so that he might be Lord of both the dead and the living. {10} Why do you pass judgment on your brother or sister? Or you, why do you despise your brother or sister? For we will all stand before the judgment seat of God. {11} For it is written, "As I live, says the Lord, every knee shall bow to me, and every tongue shall give praise to God." {12} So then, each of us will be accountable to God. {13} Let us therefore no longer pass judgment on one another, but resolve instead never to put a stumbling block or hindrance in the way of another. {14} I know and am persuaded in the Lord Jesus that nothing is unclean in itself; but it is unclean for anyone who thinks it unclean. {15} If your brother or sister is being injured by what you eat, you are no longer walking in love. Do not let what you eat cause the ruin of one for whom Christ died. {16} So do not let your good be spoken of as evil. {17} For the kingdom of God is not food and drink but righteousness and peace and joy in the Holy Spirit. {18} The one who thus serves Christ is acceptable to God and has human approval. {19} Let us then pursue what makes for peace and for mutual upbuilding. {20} Do not, for the sake of food, destroy the work of God. Everything is indeed clean, but it is wrong for you to make others fall by what you eat; {21} it is good not to eat meat or drink wine or do anything that makes your brother or sister stumble. {22} The faith that you have, have as your own conviction before God. Blessed are those who have no reason to condemn themselves because of what they approve. {23} But those who have doubts are condemned if they eat, because they do not act from faith; for whatever does not proceed from faith is sin."

This passage is too long to give full attention to, but the full length of the text allows us to explore a complete theme and some of the sub-themes that will illustrate our approach to Pauline thought. If we have identified the overall issue, that of the urge to conform to the culture, we have not yet identified the torah text that serves to clarify the obligations of the gentile Christians Paul addresses. In fact, we have in this passage only the reference to Isaiah 45 (in verse 11) as any link to the Tanach. Nevertheless, this reference is significant despite the apparently superficial way that Paul applies the reference to his argument. We will return to the Isaiah reference shortly. First, however, we must sort through what is the foundation for a gentile *halakah* that might be evident in this Romans text. In fact, we have no explicit definition of that source here in Romans except in discipleship to Jesus who is the Christ. For Paul, that link to Jesus becomes an essential step toward building a Christian lifestyle.

We do have the eventual development of the Noachide commandments that were neither clearly delineated in Rabbinic Judaism until after the time of Paul nor was the intent of the Noachide laws theologically clear. On the one hand, the rabbis seemed to think of the commands as a justification for the condemnation of the gentiles in that the commandments of God were offered to the sons of Noah (to the nations) but were rejected.[40] On the other hand, the rabbis seemed to take Paul's direction, even in one instance referring to Isaiah 45:23, in allowing for the appearance of the righteous among the nations. The seven commands (at least six were already accepted in early Pharisaic circles) could become the basis for a universal covenant. It is likely that Paul knew at least some of this tradition at an early stage of its development, and the foundation for a gentile *halakah* could be the basic commandments accepted (according to tradition) by the sons of Noah.

---

40. See the discussion in:
     Segal, *Paul the Convert*, p. 194ff.

If this is the case, then what is at stake in Romans 14? Surely two related commands are at stake in the practical matters that Paul considers in this chapter: (1) the question of idolatry and (2) the matter of profaning God's name. These two commands seem to be the issue far more than the matter of dietary laws. Indeed, it is not the belief among the rabbis that the dietary laws apply to the gentiles at all, except in the case of eating flesh that has the blood in it. Paul's reference to eating surely pertains to the command to refrain from idolatry and not to any gentile version of dietary laws. If we are correct, then surely the central issue of the urge to conform to the culture is represented here by the issue of food offered to idols (more specifically food that remained from the Roman feasts). The issue is whether conforming to the culture by eating food offered to idols is a breaking of the prohibition of idolatry.

Romans 14 is an *halakah* for gentiles in that Paul speaks to the matter of what it means to refrain from idolatry in the context of Roman culture.[41] Note that Paul's response does not prohibit the eating of the meat as gentiles are clearly not obligated to refrain from eating meat offered to idols, but rather makes the issue one of community unity. Even if some do not suffer the urge to conform to the Roman cultural religious practice in eating certain foods or in observing certain days, they should refrain from doing so for the sake of the community. Since the religious practices of Rome are not binding in any way on the gentile Christians (what they eat they eat to the Lord, giving thanks to God), this decision for the sake of the community is an important feature of resisting the ideology and cultural pressure of "the world."

Paul iterates here a precept that is clearly common in early

---

41. Tomson argues that the issue I have isolated does not fit the context of Romans 14 and suggests that the issue is fundamentally table fellowship between Jewish-Christians and Gentile-Christians. In fact, this point is worth pursuing as well, but the argument depends on a judgment I have already rejected, that Romans 14 and 15 are incidental to the theological material of especially Romans 1-11. If we reject the assumption that Tomson begins with and see that Romans 12:1 makes the key issue one of conforming or not conforming to the world, then the language of Romans 14 implies far more probably that the problem is the prohibition of idolatry. In that vein, the quotation from Isaiah 45:23 supports our case rather than refuting it as Tomson argues. See, Peter Tomson, *Paul and the Jewish Law*, pp. 236ff.

Judaism, that good deeds can be a source of salvation for another, that is, the new obligations on Christians are a witness to others, those who are weak. This precept in Pauline texts like Romans is taken in its negative side, to refrain from endangering the redemption of those who are weak, and in this case, the weak are those who are unable to withstand the pressures of the culture except by separating themselves as much as possible from culture. This, too, is a slight variation on what we find in the Rabbis. Nevertheless, it is a clear indication from the Pauline texts that salvation is a term that applies not so much to separate individuals but to the whole community. Indeed, salvation for the individual can mean little if it is viewed in competition with the health of the whole community.

That this halakic principle is central to Paul's message is undoubtable, and the principle implies that no theology could work for Paul that did not make the fate of the whole community its centerpiece. Of course, that would mean that the Christian lifestyle could never be interpreted as a disconnected independent individual life. Likewise, soteriology could never be seen as applying to an individual separated from the community since the community is the centerpiece of Christian life. No individualism or belief that living produces an individual standing before God can pass as an appropriate way of understanding Christianity.

Thus, Paul was attempting (by this reading) to build a fence around the community in a manner similar to the Rabbis. But what community do we mean by this claim? The community is the new community of the church in which both gentile followers and Jewish followers of Jesus were joined together. Now this community is not completely unique in that Jewish gatherings could often include gentile god-fearers as part of the community. That is, the notion of the righteous among the gentiles had begun to take shape in this time, and those righteous could be granted a place in the kingdom of God not by observance of the torah but by observance of the Noachide laws. That is, a precedent had already developed for Paul in building an *halakah* for the church.

The difference in the case of Romans was that the audience was not the Jewish community of the synagogue but the gentile followers of Jesus. If the principle audience is gentiles and not Jews, then we might ask what *halakah* would assure that gentiles would respect the same unity of the community that was evident among some of the growing Rabbinic view of the righteous among the gentiles. The gentiles would have to refrain from those cultural practices that would endanger the spiritual wellbeing of the Jewish followers of Jesus who could not openly participate in such a lifestyle. The whole issue of dietary laws and days of observance is linked with the necessity of safeguarding the wellbeing of the whole community.

That is to say, Paul appears to be offering a teaching of respect in place of a teaching of contempt, quite the opposite of what came to be the Pauline heritage. What makes this teaching especially valuable for a post-Shoah Christian theology is that Paul offers this *halakah* in the context of an alien culture in which the leadership was potentially hostile to the community. Thus, the appeal to be transformed rather than to conform was a call to resist the larger culture in its potential to divide and then destroy the community. Of course, we do not have complete instructions for the Romans as to how this resistance was to be carried out, only that whatever was done be done to the glory of God. Perhaps Paul believed that a more developed set of rules for living would be established by the leaders of the community recognizing the need for such a fence around the community.

Of course, the horror of the Shoah challenges Christian living on precisely the level we have been speaking. If the aim of a regime is to divide and destroy the community, then is it better to simply comply or to resist? Christians have a mixed record to look back upon during the Shoah. Even in the name of protecting the wellbeing of the community, churches often decided to comply out of fear. Even more, the churches were not able to distinguish themselves from the culture sufficiently to be able to ask the questions that Paul asks.[42] That is, the precept of resistance that appears in Romans 12 is absent from the ongoing lifestyle of Christians in Nazi Germany as well as most other places in our modern world.

There can be little doubt that an operating *halakah* on eating and observance of holy days would have created more immediate conflict between the church and Nazi ideology than was apparent among most of the churches. Still, the sense of a teaching of respect remained as a vestige

---

42. Of course, any full treatment of the Pauline material must look at Romans 13 in the light of our claim. Surely Paul does counsel cooperation with ruling authority in chapter 13, but the question remains what is the situation that leads Paul to this counsel. The *halakah* always develops from a context that demands a response. However, we cannot take up this matter in this paper, unfortunately.

of the Pauline theme and formed a basis for some of the most active resistance.[43] I would argue that any post-Shoah Christian theology must develop the Pauline trajectory toward an *halakah* on these matters which means moving Christian reflection from central theological tenets toward the demands of Christian living. Such a transformation of the habits of Christian theology might be nearly impossible, but the test of whether a post-Shoah Christian theology is possible might depend on our ability to do that.

THE DIALOGUE COMMUNITY

The teaching of respect that we have implied is at least a viable interpretation of the Pauline halakic material works well if it is developed and accepted in the community. That is, it can be a means for building a fence around the community of the church (even if the church now has no sign of a remnant of Jewish followers of Jesus since the message is aimed toward Paul's gentile readers.) This teaching would develop into an effective weapon of resistance to cultural forces that threaten to divide and destroy the community. However, we have no direct guarantee that that respect would also be extended to those outside of the community, namely to the living Jewish community. And, after all, it is the relation of gentile Christians to Jews that is the lingering cloud hanging over Christianity after the Shoah. Unless, we can shape an *halakah* for that relationship, can we have a genuine post-Shoah Christian community?

Of course, we do not need Paul to respond to the need for a new

---

43. Connections made between Christian understanding of scripture and the acts of resistance and rescue during the Shoah are difficult to make with assurance, even though studies show that Christians from Calvinist background, where particular rules for living, derived from scripture, are more central to the community's self-understanding, might have been more inclined to see resistance and rescue as a natural extension of their actions. Studies on rescue and altruism can give background to such claims, such as:

Philip Friedman, *Their Brother's Keepers* (New York: Schocken Books, 1978);

Philip Hallie, *Lest Innocent Blood Be Shed* (San Francisco: Harper and Row, 1979); and

S.P. Oliner and P.M. Oliner, *The Altruistic Personality* (New York: The Free Press, 1988).

halakah concerning Christian-Jewish relations. However, unless such an *halakah* is rooted in Christian scripture, it is doubtful that such a basic rule for Christian living can become widely accepted in the church. It is this problematic that continues to plague the dialogue in our time. While much has been said about the need for a new kind of understanding about a Christian view of Judaism (and some of the thinkers that are part of the spectrum I posed above), the problem is making these gains from dialogue a central fixture of Christian teaching and living, that is, reaching the laypeople who sit in the pews in the churches.

In fact, Pauline thought is both seen as a potential resource and as the chief problem in accomplishing this new way of thinking and acting. It is in Romans that Paul addresses the issue of the relation between the church and Judaism in such a way that many scholars find the ingredients for a new view in those chapters (Romans 9-11). On the other hand, Paul's understanding of the law, particularly, his position on circumcision represent the most difficult barriers facing us as we try to alter the impressions left from centuries of teaching these words of Paul. Again, I am confining my reflections at this point to Romans although the problem arising from the Pauline material is at least as critical in other letters from Paul. What we aim for though is an illustration of an approach, an halakic approach that moves in the reverse direction from much of Pauline interpretation.

The Audience

The problem in judging whether Romans is a resource or not rests with deciding about who the audience for Paul's letters is. We have followed Stendahl and Gaston in arguing that the audience is the gentile church and that Paul aims to construct an *halakah* for the new gentile Christians.[44]   Many scholars are not convinced by that way of understanding Paul (e.g., Alan Segal),[45] but our intent is not to present exegetical warrants for our theology but to ask how we can read Paul so as to retrieve the text for a post-Shoah Christian theology. That is, we build from a view that holds that any text presents a plurality of possible

---

44. See especially, Lloyd Gaston, *Paul and the Torah*, chapter 2.

    Also, Krister Stendahl, *Paul Among Jews and Gentiles* Philadelphia: Fortress Press, 1976).

45. See, Alan Segal, *Paul the Convert.*

interpretations and theological applications and we should choose a reading that is most adequate to the demands of a post-Shoah theology. We may still discover that we cannot retrieve Pauline thought for those purposes as Rosemary Ruether warns; however the approach that we have suggested has potential for a fresh reading of Paul that opens the door for new directions in Christian thinking.

Thus, we continue to argue that the most productive reading of the Pauline material arises from accepting Gaston's claim that Paul nearly exclusively aims his comments to the gentile church.[46] We have seen that reading Romans 14 in this way can help us to unfold a teaching of respect built into Paul's understanding of Christian living, a position that reverses some of the way that Pauline material has been used in the past. Our problem is not that Paul presents a teaching of contempt, for that seems not to be the case even with the obvious polemic in some of his material, but whether his potential teaching of respect builds a way of Christian thinking and living that extends beyond the relation of gentiles and Jews in the church. It is one thing to instruct gentile Christians to be transformed in order to safeguard the integrity of the new Christian community, that is to respect the practices of Jewish Christians in that community, but quite another to build a *halakah* that includes gentile attitudes toward non-Christians, specifically the Jewish community. But this question continues to focus our attention on the gentile Christians and Paul's halakic instruction for them.

The Question of Circumcision and Abraham

Romans 4 includes a remarkable series of references to the Torah that are woven together in a careful argument concerning the matter of righteousness and the question of circumcision. While Paul's position in Roman's is clearly less polemic than, for example, a similar passage in Galatians, the passage can be taken as a supercessionist view of Christianity. The text can be read as an answer to the question we have been raising, that Judaism stands outside of the community of the righteous because righteousness comes through God's gift because of faith. Romans 4 appears to be the consummate expression of Paul's gospel of faith and Paul's rejection of Judaism. That is, if the chapter were seen as a development of a theology, this reading of the text could be appropriate.

---

46. Gaston, *Paul and the Torah*, p. 20ff.

Let me put the text before us.

> {4:1} What then are we to say was gained by Abraham, our ancestor according to the flesh? {2} For if Abraham was justified by works, he has something to boast about, but not before God. {3} For what does the scripture say? "Abraham believed God, and it was reckoned to him as righteousness." {4} Now to one who works, wages are not reckoned as a gift but as something due. {5} But to one who without works trusts him who justifies the ungodly, such faith is reckoned as righteousness. {6} So also David speaks of the blessedness of those to whom God reckons righteousness apart from works: {7} "Blessed are those whose iniquities are forgiven, and whose sins are covered; {8} blessed is the one against whom the Lord will not reckon sin." {9} Is this blessedness, then, pronounced only on the circumcised, or also on the uncircumcised? We say, "Faith was reckoned to Abraham as righteousness." {10} How then was it reckoned to him? Was it before or after he had been circumcised? It was not after, but before he was circumcised. {11} He received the sign of circumcision as a seal of the righteousness that he had by faith while he was still uncircumcised. The purpose was to make him the ancestor of all who believe without being circumcised and who thus have righteousness reckoned to them, {12} and likewise the ancestor of the circumcised who are not only circumcised but who also follow the example of the faith that our ancestor Abraham had before he was circumcised. {13} For the promise that he would inherit the world did not come to Abraham or to his descendants through the law but through the righteousness of faith. {14} If it is the adherents of the law who are to be the heirs, faith is null and the promise is void. {15} For the law brings wrath; but where there is no law, neither is there violation. {16} For this reason it depends on faith, in order that the promise may rest on grace and be guaranteed to all his descendants, not only to the adherents of the law but also to those who share the faith of Abraham (for he is the father of all of us, {17} as it is written, "I have made you the father of many nations")—in the presence of the God in whom he believed, who gives life to the dead and calls into existence the things that do not exist. {18} Hoping against hope, he believed that he would become "the father of many nations," according to what was said, "So numerous shall your descendants be." {19} He did not weaken in faith when he considered his own body, which was already as good as dead (for he was about a hundred years old), or when he considered the barrenness of Sarah's womb. {20} No distrust made him waver concerning the promise of God, but he grew strong in his faith as he gave glory to God, {21} being fully convinced that God was able to do what he had

promised. {22} Therefore his faith "was reckoned to him as righteousness." {23} Now the words, "it was reckoned to him," were written not for his sake alone, {24} but for ours also. It will be reckoned to us who believe in him who raised Jesus our Lord from the dead, {25} who was handed over to death for our trespasses and was raised for our justification.

Now this chapter is again a complex text requiring careful development that we cannot fully provide. Nevertheless, we can do what we have done thus far; we can offer hints about how an interpretation might be approached. If the central concern of Romans is that of Romans 12:1-2 that we quoted above, then the issue is not essentially the relation between Christianity and Judaism but rather the threat of syncretism in the church and the impact of that on Christian living. Thus, Romans can be perceived as an *halakah* which aims to provide instructions for living in a hostile cultural environment. If Paul were merely speaking to a gentile church in Rome, however, the retreat to the story of Abraham would have quite a different meaning than if the church were still struggling with the mixing of gentiles and Jewish Christians in a single community. There would not be a problem with circumcision because Judaism did not demand circumcision of righteous gentiles. Paul had no need to give a different instruction. On this matter there would be no conflict between the convert Paul and the Jewish community (even Jewish Christians).

But the issue clearly is circumcision and for the reason that Paul's vision of a Christian community included Jews and Gentiles together, eating and worshipping together. We have seen his instruction for gentiles in the matter of eating and observance, a matter that surely can become for us a theme for dialogue, but the issue of circumcision arises on the level of the formation of the community itself, indeed, of the legitimacy of the gentile mission of Paul. On the issue of circumcision, then, Paul must speak not only to the gentiles giving them an *halakah* on this matter but must speak to the Jewish followers of Jesus who were part of the community. That is, Paul must speak about the relationship between Christians and Jews in order to clarify this gentile *halakah*.

It is this necessity that leads Paul to Genesis and to the Abraham story. It is interesting that Paul chooses to turn to Genesis and not to Exodus, Leviticus and Deuteronomy, other references to the practice of circumcision. By choosing the Abraham story, Paul deliberately returns to an era before the giving of the Sinai covenant and thus before the creation of the people of Israel, the people of the covenant. With Abraham, Paul chooses a figure who pre-dates the naming of Jacob and the creation of the family of Israel. With Abraham, Paul chooses the father of both the line of Israel and the peoples of the nations. Abraham is the one place in the Torah where the relation between Israel and the nations is still an open matter. It is not surprising that Paul should turn to Abraham for all of these reasons, but of course the story of Abraham is the principal source for the practice of circumcision and the logical place to turn. Paul interprets the text that is the heart of the matter.

Still, it is not the whole story but specific verses that Paul attempts to apply to the issue at hand[47], not in the style of modern exegesis but in an *halakic* style. The issue is righteousness and the problem to be solved is what to do about circumcision. Paul argues, using Genesis 15:6, that Abraham was declared righteous because of his trust in God. That is, circumcision, which is commanded in Genesis 17:10, comes after God's declaring Abraham righteous. Circumcision, thereby, is seen as a sign of faith and not merely as a commandment of the covenant. If the latter were so, then all people of Abraham's flesh, including the nations, would be commanded by God to circumcise. This is the puzzle of Paul's argument since he appears to move in the direction of loosening the command to circumcise but makes an argument that seems to imply the importance of circumcision all the more. Even if it is faith that is central and the heart of righteousness (this thought is consistent with Paul's comments in Romans 3), the sign is still obviously the public acknowledgement of that faith commanded by God. In fact, the focus on faith does not lessen but heightens the importance of circumcision.

In Romans, Paul does not reject circumcision or the circumcised. Indeed, he implies that those who are like Abraham, that is trusting in God, are all under God's mercy. The circumcised do not, in this line of thought, need Jesus to put them close to God. It is clear from this chapter that Paul has left the door open for two unique expressions of Abraham's faith - the children of Abraham who became the children of Israel and the children of Abraham who are drawn to God through faith in Jesus as the

---

47. We note that Paul does not interpret in the style of the Rabbis by quoting the sages and applying them to the issue except for his reference to the Psalms. Still, this too is not surprising if Paul believed that he was making a new thing, a gentile *halakah*, that the Rabbis would not have had as their concern.

Christ. And thus we have the ingredients for a different kind of Pauline theology which is fundamentally a teaching of respect like what we saw in Romans 14. Abraham can be counted as the father of both the uncircumcised of the nations who believe through Christ and of the circumcised who follow the example of Abraham, the example of Abraham's trust.[48]

Of course, this point only reinforces what is true anyway, that the Rabbis were moving toward a view of the righteous among the nations that basically matches Paul's view. But Paul is doing something new here; he is constructing a gentile *halakah* which must have a different aim than the intention of the Rabbis. Paul's message is not aimed at the Jewish community, even though there are clearly implications for Jews, but at the church, specifically at the gentile church. It is for that reason, we might argue, that Paul begins his discussion by centering on the issue of righteousness and with the aim of addressing the larger issue of living in a hostile cultural environment. Indeed, if Paul's argument is correct about Abraham, then the problem for gentiles is a false pride, that they can be counted as righteous even without circumcision. Indeed, the fact that to live without circumcision meant that gentiles could more easily manage in the Roman culture was surely not lost on Paul. Circumcision was precisely the public sign that made Jews vulnerable either to cultural pressure or to exposure, at least as threatening as the special dietary laws and the commands regarding the observance of holy days.

Gentile Christians were in less danger than their Jewish counterparts unless they openly associated with Jewish followers of Jesus. That is to say, the issue of circumcision was at least as divisive in the Christian community as the dietary laws not for the reasons often suggested but because the key issue in Rome was not conforming to the culture but being transformed by God. Gentile Christians needed an *halakah* to guard against this threat to apostasy, to insidious pride, that could tear the new churches apart. Gentiles were challenged by Paul not to boast because the grace of God comes not as a result of their special work but because of faith, the one who trusts the God who justifies the ungodly. And what is this *halakah* for the gentiles?

---

48. This focus on trust which appears as a central theme for Berkovits in *With God in Hell* is both a bridge to conversation between what I am doing with Paul and Berkovits' reflections on the actuality of a Holocaust *halakah* as well as an invitation for dialogue on this point between Christians and Jews.

We are now led back to the one interpretive passage that Paul brings to his understanding of Abraham's faith, a text that seems at first to be completely out of place. Indeed, the text of Psalm 32 that Paul uses refers not to what is given and declared by God as gift but to what is not reckoned, that is the sin of the one who confesses. The reference seems more in tune with sin offering than with Abraham's story and certainly has little to do with circumcision. Indeed, the passage has more to do with righteousness, that is the life that is right with God. But of course, that is the focus of Paul's thinking in Romans 4. The resolution of what to do about circumcision centers on what is the heart of the righteous life. The text in Psalm 32 is all the more remarkable as it is a text that the Rabbis see as messianic, as an expression of the messianic age. The heart of the righteous life is the fear of God expressed in confession of sin. The only way to temper pride is to turn the gentile church toward confession. Regular confession of sin for Paul links the gentiles to the story of Abraham and thus to the share we have with Jews in the glory of God (indeed, the very words that follow in Romans 5).

Of course, it is the focus on forgiveness that allows Paul to argue for a community in which both gentiles and Jews can eat together in their own way. It is the confession of sin that allows the gentile church to recall its roots in Abraham and to re-focus its teaching on a teaching of respect for Jews rather than of contempt (pride). That Psalm 32 links also to the vision of the messianic community is by no means an accident. The sort of unity Paul saw in the relationship here implied is messianic. The cultures we are part of will always tend to threaten the messianic vision by calling for conformity and wiping out diversity. Paul's vision focussed on confession and the glory of God's mercy calls for transforming the mind in a vision of unity that respects diversity. This is his message to the gentile church, a message, I believe, is echoed in Romans 11, the text so often debated concerning Paul's views of Judaism.

But this is the focus that is so challenged by the Shoah. Perhaps we must finally say that focus on the Christ, on the messiah, produced not the vision I have suggested resides in Paul's *halakah* but in a pride of contempt toward the Jew as Rosemary Ruether has argued. The messianic vision became focussed not so much in confession as in reward, the claim to righteousness. Perhaps Paul's *halakah* has failed for no matter what we might claim is Paul's intent, the result has produced the apostasy of the twentieth century. And if the *halakah* failed during the Shoah can it be valid for Christians in a post-Shoah theology? This is a serious challenge to the heart of Christianity. Apostasy is difficult enough to come to terms with, but can we tolerate apostasy produced by the heart of Christian belief?

Returning to Berkovits and Retrieving the *Halakah*

What we have done with the Pauline material is very preliminary having considered only one portion of one book of the Pauline corpus. Considering the enormous impact of Pauline thought on both Christian theology and on Christian attitudes toward Jews, much more is needed to work through the many issues that would enable us to retrieve Pauline thought for a post-Shoah Christian theology. Still, we have suggested an approach that makes the work ahead clearer for us. At least we would want to argue that the best, perhaps the only, way to retrieve Pauline thought for post-Shoah Christians is to see Paul as developing an *halakah* for gentile Christians. In doing so, Paul identified what it is to be a Christian in an alien setting, in a culture that was not receptive, even hostile to being a Christian.

In that sense, we can argue with some confidence that Paul did not see Christianity as a replacement for Judaism at all. In fact, the minimal work we have done seems to take great pains to define gentile Christianity in a way quite distinct from Pharisaic Judaism, in a way similar to the way the Rabbis would speak of the righteous gentiles. Thus, gentiles are not commanded to follow the Jewish dietary laws or the observance of the Jewish days of worship but they are commanded to avoid idolatry and to maintain the unity of the whole community of Christians. Also, gentiles are not commanded to circumcise because that is a sign of the covenant with Israel, but are rather invited to show their commitment through public confession in the community. In short, Paul defines the *halakah* for gentiles in a way that prepares for a teaching of respect for others and a shared mission with Jews (a notion that seems to be the thrust of Paul's comments in Romans 11).

All of these conclusions need to be tested in relation to the larger Pauline corpus partly because the same issues are consistently pursued for Christians in other places than Rome and because we cannot assume that Paul viewed each church as facing the same critical issue of conformity to the culture. However, we must move forward to ask the harder question about whether this halakic understanding allows for a retrieval of Pauline thought in a post-Shoah world. This question is too extensive to be managed in this paper, but we can make a start with our response to this matter as well, especially if we return to where we began, with Eliezer Berkovits.

Berkovits, we recall, argues that the viability of post-Shoah judgments, particularly about the faith of individuals and the validity of Jewish observance during the Shoah, is questionable. The only way that we can understand the value of Judaism as a lifestyle for the Shoah is to listen to testimonies from survivors and victims. Even as we do that, however, our judgments can be skewed because the testimonies are surely mixed and memories are not always clear. So the issue becomes whether a minimalist claim might be sustained, whether Judaism not only was viable for some but because of the observance of that remnant is preserved for the next generation. This is a bold argument offered by Berkovits because he for one understands fully the twist that the Shoah gave to the whole matter of religious observance. Thus, viability is not so much a test of whether some managed to observe all the *halakah* that applied but whether the *halakah* itself was flexible enough to be transformed to meet this new, horrendous, unique situation in the history of Judaism. That is, Berkovits' test concerns the halakic approach and not merely the specific *halakah*.

In fact, Berkovits is quite persuasive concerning this issue. We are not fully convinced that he answers all critics who ask what is left of this trust in the tradition, or more specifically in the God of the tradition when so many have died, even those who were faithful in every way they could, Irving Greenberg's challenge. To preserve a tradition for the sake of such a minimally successful argument is questionable, for the very reasons that Victor Frankl and Bruno Bettelheim gave. That is, the bare minimum of the *halakah* was sufficiently preserved, but for what purpose other than merely preserving. The answer for Berkovits is linked to his own continuing messianic vision, his own orthodoxy. Either he will cling to the trust (the *emunah*) that the righteous will be rewarded, the messianic hope, or he can argue that the survival of Judaism is a survival of Judaism's righteous mission to heal the world, which is Emil Fackenheim's conclusion. Perhaps the two hopes are inseparable for Berkovits and I suspect he holds to the truth of both.

Now Berkovits has little concern about demonstrating the viability of Christianity after the Shoah. He may, in fact, feel that such an argument is not possible and at any rate should not be attempted by Jews. He may not be appreciative of Irving Greenberg's efforts to do just that. Still, the pattern that Berkovits provides is an indicator of the next stage of our important work. If a midrashic approach to Christian scripture, particularly the Christian gospel stories, provides a new *aggadah* for teaching and preaching that is truly a post-Shoah Christian theology, as we have argued elsewhere,[49] then the same sort of approach to the Pauline material (as well as some of the other material in the Christian scripture) could produce an halakah for preaching and teaching, that is a truly post-Shoah pattern for Christian living. But we must do as Berkovits does; we must ask whether the halakic approach was sufficient to sustain Christian life decisions during the Shoah, a task made more difficult because the halakic approach has not been the way that Christians have conceived their teaching and practice even if, in fact, such an *halakah* has always been in place.

This is also a minimalist claim that can fully recognize that the Christian way of living was not viable for a variety of reasons for a great many people. Franklin Littell has referred to this fact as the great Christian apostasy and he may be correct in that assessment.[50] But apostasy is not a pattern for living even if we can fully understand the causes, and apostasy does not preserve let alone retrieve a valid gentile *halakah* for us or for those who faced what we have not, the horror of the Shoah. If this was the only testimony that has survived for us, then we could not pretend to make even a minimalist claim for Christianity. At that, our argument will be vulnerable to the same charge that is leveled by Frankl and Bettelheim, for what good does a minimal religious tradition survive. Our answer remains the same as that of Berkovits, we present this argument not for the sake of the mere tradition but for the sake of preserving the messianic vision, the twofold hope for the reward of the righteous and the mission of healing the world.

Now this, for gentiles like us, can only be a shared mission, a mission that begins in a teaching of respect. But now we know that respect that leads to the kind of resistance to the ravages of alien culture that is at the heart of Paul's concern for the new Christian church cannot be merely managed by a transformation in our teaching or even in believing that our teaching will eventually transform our behavior. We need more than stories that teach respect, we need an *halakah*, a fence around the tradition, that instructs us for a life that expresses respect. We need more than the integral need to resist; we need an ethic of rescue. This is an ethic that not only teaches gentiles that through Christ we are called to respect Jews but

---

49. James Moore, *Christian Theology After the Shoah*, p. 75ff.

50. Franklin Littell, *The Crucifixion of the Jews* (Macon, Ga: Mercer University Press, 1975), p. 75ff.

also through this same Christ we are called to help preserve Judaism in its uniqueness, in its role as a part of God's messianic mission.

We, therefore, ask whether there is a testimony for such an *halakah* and those who have worked hard at recording these testimonies have prepared the way for this companion piece of our work. The point is not whether Paul or any other leading Christian thinker had given an instruction that could prepare the way for such rescue. That seems dubious and we would not retrieve Paul because we thought so simplistically as that. Rather we ask whether the halakic approach to the Christian tradition allowed for the *halakah* of rescue to emerge even in spite of the tremendous pressure to beat it back and kill it. I suspect, even though I cannot present the case now, that such an argument can be made using the work of those who have interviewed the rescuers. Our problem is not finding the testimony, at least not for now, but that a pattern is difficult to establish. Perhaps a pattern is impossible given the unique terror of the Shoah, but we fear that the pattern will mean nothing unless it is firmly established in the teaching of the church. That is, we cannot be certain that rescuers would appear in the future, but we can now see more clearly the necessity of this ethic of rescue, specifically as that relates to Jewish-Christian relations.

Conclusion

I have already presented more in this paper than is normal for such presentations. Thus, we must close prematurely knowing that the work is only opened up to us and needs so much more to complete. We have, I believe, seen a new kind of work for the new generation, however. We have a fresh approach to the whole matter of interpretation of Christian scripture for the sake of developing a post-Shoah Christian theology. We have set for ourselves yet another mission of not only a Christian midrash but also a Christian *halakah* that must arise in our post-Shoah thinking and living. Some of the particulars that have emerged from our treatment of sections of Romans might have significant importance on their own and could become fruit for our discussions together. I am struck particularly by the instruction to continue in confession and its application to a post-Shoah age. But these matters require the larger community and cannot be merely the thinking of one individual. That community, of course, must now be the community in dialogue and much of what we have said concerning Paul opens up to contribution from our Jewish dialogue partners. Thus, the incompleteness of this work is as it should be, open for the dialogue that suffers only when it is closed off too early or cannot open again to the new challenges.   That is, it is strongest when it is *halakic*.   And this incompleteness is an appropriate reminder that this work has only just begun. That is, the questions that remain and the ideas that are only just taking shape are an invitation to join this work, dare we say messianic work?!

Chapter 3: The *Akeda* in Dialogue: Reading Scripture Together After the Shoah

For reasons that I hope become abundantly clear, I will confine my reflections to a small portion of Genesis 22 (verses 1 and 2) as a way to read the rest of the text. In addition, I will conduct this analysis in relation to a companion text in the Christian scriptures, John 3:16, also for reasons that should become obvious. Most importantly, I contend that reading these two texts together will help highlight my approach to a new Christian theology that takes the form of a midrashic reading.[1] Ordinarily, I argue that Christian texts can be better understood by thinking of them as midrash, that is, as commentary on the Torah tradition. A full reading of Christian texts, then, requires making the full connection with Torah texts. However, because of the nature of this session, I am reversing the procedure in order to allow a Christian text to give insight into how one might read a Torah text. Even as I do this, however, I will be applying certain theological criteria that make of our reading a post-Shoah theological understanding of texts. Briefly, those criteria are (1) that all theology must be dialogical, respecting the views of our Jewish dialogue partners in their own right; (2) that all theology must be post-Shoah bringing to bear the most difficult questions raised by the tremendum of the Shoah about our religious views; and (3) that all theology must be hermeneutical applying the meaning of texts to the real situations of contemporary religious people and communities. This latter point may mean more appropriately that theology is homiletical, a difference we can spend time discussing if need be.

The two verses of Genesis 22 that I focus on are as follows: "After these things God tested Abraham. He said to him, "Abraham!" And he said, "Here I am." He said, "Take your son, your only son Isaac, whom you love, and go to the land of Moriah, and offer him there as a burnt offering on one of the mountains that I shall show you. (NRSV) For our reference let me

---

[1] James Moore, *Christian Theology after the Shoah* (Lanham, Md: University Press of America, 1993).

also give the text from John 3:16: "For God so loved the world that he gave his only Son, so that everyone who believes in him may not perish but may have eternal life." (NRSV)

At least for a short time, it is worth thinking about my claim that the verse from John is potentially a midrash on Genesis 22. At least theologically, the structure of the story of the *akeda* and the story of the gospel are similar. That is, Christian theology has implied that God's act to offer the Son is parallel to the offering commanded of Abraham. Jesus is seen as the only son, as a type of Isaac. Thus, we could hardly understand this Christian text fully unless we come to terms with the meaning of the Genesis text. This midrashic reading of John is made even more crucial if we agree that the single verse from the Gospel of John we have quoted represents a nutshell summary of central Christian belief. Of course, these are sweeping claims which can be but will not be defended here. It is perhaps fruitful to keep in mind that such a reading of John is possible and may suggest several interesting possibilities to us as we unfold our reading of Genesis.

What I want to do though is think about the meaning of Genesis 22 as that can be understood, using John 3:16 as a tool to open up avenues of thinking. Most essentially, I look to explore the meaning in context of the words *nissah* (test), *achavta* (the beloved), and *yichiddah* (the only one). All of these words are ambiguous in their present context and require a sorting through possibilities in order to assess their meaning. In the end, the words may elude our efforts to make their meaning definite and their very ambiguity may prove fruitful for a post-Shoah theology. These words are also quite important in this context as they relate to the idea of *olah* (burnt offering) that is also ambiguous and surely disturbing given our own memory of the Shoah. That is to say, it is precisely the inter-connection between the ideas of test, of election, of love and of burnt offering that so disturbs us today.

NISSAH (TEST)

Anyone who works with languages realizes that the meaning of words is contextual, and that is especially true of the Hebrew Scriptures. The older versions of translation of this word render it as tempt. Even that translation remains ambiguous since this verse has God doing the tempting either to test (whether Abraham would choose wrongly) or to lead (enticing Abraham to go a particular direction). Even more, the notion that God would tempt seems out of character with the more consistent understanding of God in the Hebrew Bible. Thus, I have translated the term as test (as do most of the more recent translations). Nevertheless, the word test also is ambiguous and requires some explication.

There are two ways that test is used in the Bible that I suggest do not ultimately fit this story even though they might be applied by some people as a way of reading this verse. First, the story could be read as a challenge (in a way, like the people of Israel tested God in the wilderness), that is as a roadblock to determine whether Abraham was on the right track with God. I take it that Paul in his use of the Abraham stories might have seen the test as just this and thus sees Abraham's obedience as a sign that Abraham was on track, the track that the whole people of God should be on. Paul takes Abraham to be a type. I am not inclined to accept this view as persuasive since the act of obedience seems not to be on track but rather leads to an act that is both an abomination and finally a destruction of the promise given to Abraham. Putting this challenge before Abraham does not make sense of the other particulars of this story even if this meaning is often the way the story is understood.

A second possible meaning for this word is that it is a test of Abraham's faith, that is, the whole exercise is meant to solidify Abraham's commitment to God and make it true. Again, this way of understanding the word seems quite common. In a way such a reading would make the whole story merely symbolic of the proper relationship between God and humans. Perhaps the apostle Paul implies some of this meaning as well. It is not a real test, then, since Abraham would never have believed that God would require the offering, but is rather a symbol of Abraham's trust in God. Such typologies render the reality of the whole situation ludicrous and do not take seriously the story as event. If we did that we would have to ask why such a command would be used (if nothing else for the sake of Isaac and Sarah) to prove Abraham's commitment. Why do we require the suffering of others to prove our faith?

In fact, our challenge of this approach to the narrative, to see the story as a test of Abraham, is a critical interpretive decision. If not a test of Abraham, what then of the whole idea of divine testing of the people of God? If not a test of Abraham, for whom is this a test? I have not really given an argument for abandoning this traditional interpretation, only some questions about its propriety. Once having opened the question, though, we are led to at least one possible conclusion, that the commands of God cannot really be seen as tests. That is, the notion of testing implied in this way of looking at the divine-human relation is not fitting for whatever else we know of that relationship. The point may well be that the divine command is never so utterly clear so as to elicit such automatic obedience, not from Abraham who so vociferously challenges Yahweh on the matter of Sodom. Thus, commands become issues to be debated in the community and not merely individual fiats for action. If this is the case, then we can look at the whole idea of divine commands and the Shoah in a different light.

But if this is not a test of Abraham, then it must be a test of God. Is this not strange, even laughable? Why would God set a test for Godself and place it before a human for the sake of resolving that test? Why would God trust Abraham to carry out his part? This is, indeed, a troubling question but one that seems pressed upon us at any rate, that the God of this narrative is one who proves Godself in the human realm. As a Christian, I am led to see this notion tied to a Christian way of understanding Jesus, and that connection may help us see critical features of this story of Abraham, Isaac and God, especially if, as I would claim, the Jesus narrative implies the same thing, that God plays out a test of Godself in and through this human, Jesus -- "God loved the world so much that God gave God's only Son."(John 3:16)

Having set up this connection, I can offer two companion narratives that speak of testing -- the story of the temptation of Jesus and the story of Gethsemane. There may be other possible examples but these two narratives strike me as informative. Let me take only the first of these as I have treated the latter rather thoroughly elsewhere.[2] We ask of the temptation narrative, first, if this story actually depicts a test of Jesus. On a theological level, that seems highly unlikely in that the plot of the whole gospel narrative assumes that God has already invested Godself in the whole life of Jesus. When the narrative reads that Jesus is led into the wilderness for forty days to be tempted, then we suggest that the notion of testing be read differently. The Greek word used in two forms in this narrative is the same Greek word used in the Septuagint in the narrative of Abraham and Isaac. If we read these two stories in conjunction, we are led to several interesting conclusions, especially if now we see the test as a test of God brought about by God, that is whether God is actually and fully committed to this plan of action.

The temptation narrative also includes a reference to Deuteronomy 6:16 - "You shall not put the Lord your God to the **test** -- as a response to Satan's use of Psalm 91 -- having to do with bringing angels to care and protect God's people. That is to say, on the matter of whether God actually faithfully carries out God's promises, the people are not to test God. This,

---

[2] Ibid. Moore, p. 75ff.

then, is not a test of God posed by humans (or the evil one in this case). If there is a test (Jesus was led to be tempted) it is God's test of Godself. And this is the ambiguity of our human status in the midst of God's working out of God's plans. Since we cannot test God accurately, we are left with choosing to do whatever we think is Godly. Our choices, however, cannot be considered a test since the previous issue is God's, that is whether God is fully committed to this plan -- using humans to carry out divine purposes.

We are thrust back into the Genesis narrative, then, with the need to apply this point to that narrative. If the test set before Abraham is not a test of Abraham but God's choosing to test Godself, then the following narrative must be seen as giving fuller explanation of what that plan and the test imply for God and humanity. But why does God need such a test of Godself? That is a perplexing question if we view God as essentially removed from the creative order, that is, we view God's connection to humanity as such, as a choice. Now this point makes this text precisely a turning point in our understanding of God's connection to humanity, perhaps a development of the whole idea that humans were created in the divine image. The *akeda* seems to suggest that God is essentially tied to humanity in relationship and God's involving Godself in the affairs of this world is not an abstract choice but is essential to God as God. This text is a revelation of this critical characteristic of the God that is taught by the Biblical tradition. For me, that insight comes in part because of the way that the Jesus narrative gives a spin on the Hebrew Bible, and on this particular passage and its words.

Then, what is the test? One possibility is that the test is God's ultimate commitment to Abraham's people as the humans through whom God works. The only way that such a test could really be set forth is to command the sacrifice of the son, the son of Abraham. The question lingers whether this test is just, especially for the humans involved, even with the apparent choices already made by those humans. That question remains and continues to trouble us since we must be troubled by the long range implication that those whom God chooses will suffer consequences that they cannot possibly conceive. But the direction of this interpretation is that this text is a turning point in God's plan, a test of Godself, once completed becomes binding. As a result, as a Christian I must say that to take the narrative of Jesus seriously, I am compelled to accept the promises to Abraham's people as binding. The Jesus narrative depends on the finality of the *akeda* in order to be acceptable.

The issue becomes, then, how committed is God? To explore this point requires turning to the other words of the narrative that I have set aside

to discuss, the words from the second verse of the text. To do this, we will
see, leads us as Christians toward a comparison between this text and John
3:16, but now toward meanings that might have been previously obscured.
 Also to do this requires a shift in issue since we not only are led to explore
the finality of God's commitment to Godself but are also led to explore the
quality of that commitment as it pertains to humans, that is, to look closely
at the words "only" and "love."

ACHAVTAH (The One Loved)

The idea of the beloved son is not isolated to this text, but the full
meaning of the word is likely contextual. That is, the word has such a variety
of meanings within the Bible that we depend on context to give us clues here.
 Still, it is just that context that forces an ambiguity onto the meaning of this
word.   Commentators argue that it is only at the naming of Isaac that
Abraham is clear about which son is meant. Isaac is not the only beloved
son of Abraham. Thus, we are suspicious already about why this theme is
introduced into the narrative. We have a number of options which have been
limited considerably by our twist on the notion of "test" given above. We
have, for example, eliminated the existential reading of the text that has so
enticed other commentators (e.g., Kierkegaard's reflections on Abraham,
Trible's reflections on Sarah, Wiesel's reflections on Isaac).[3] Nevertheless,
since we have argued that the focus is more likely on God than Abraham
(which means also more on God than on Isaac), this existential rendering is
not our first option for understanding the text and this reference.
The idea of the beloved is introduced to clarify the test that God has
set before Godself. If that claim is at all reasonable, then we are given a
different entree into this section of the narrative. In what sense, we ask, does
God need to consider the beloved son. In this case, the answer seems to
point us to the question of election, to the one chosen. That is, the reference
to the beloved son is a symbol of God's election of Israel. To be sure, this
idea is transported to the messianic tradition, the kings of Israel also being
named the beloved son. Surely, this line of thinking stands behind the
passage in John 3:16 and to references at Jesus' baptism. This notion of the

---

[3] cf., Soren Kierkegaard, *Fear and Trembling, The Sickness Unto Death* (New
York: Doubleday, 1954), pp. 26ff.
Phyllis Trible, "Genesis 22: The Sacrifice of Sarah" *Gross Memorial Lecture*
(Valparaiso, IN: Valparaiso University, 1989)
 Elie Wiesel, *Messengers of God* (New York: Summit Books, 1976), p. 69ff.

beloved is a qualifier that further emphasizes that the test for God is a test of the choice, the election of Abraham. We will see this issue arise again when we think about the reference to the only son.

Even so, the naming of the beloved son is also a qualitative statement, but the issue remains consistent. Isaac is called the beloved not because of Abraham's choices but because of God's choice. The issue, here, is the nature of God's relation to God's choices. The qualifier is love. The issue for us is similar to the one we just discussed regarding the test. The issue is whether love is God's choice (God chooses to love this one) or the choice is made because God loves. The text seems to tilt us to the latter even though the qualifier is still ambiguous to us. If God is love, then the choice to work through humans, specifically Abraham and his progeny, is a natural extension of God's essence.

It is just this issue that we see at stake in John 3:16. Notice that the whole scene is now qualified by the phrase "God loved the *world*." That is, the Christian text now reads election as rooted in God's love for the whole world and not in the particular love of Isaac. This means two things at least. First, God acts to redeem for the sake of all and the issue about whether Isaac or Ishmael is bypassed here. God's actions are not merely dependent on whether God loves or even whether God loves especially this one. God's love is taken to be foundational and in that requires the redemptive activity that follows. Thus, the whole narrative of Abraham is read to be the initiation of a redemptive process (a *tikkun olam*) for which the election of Abraham is essential. Second, election itself is the issue here, but the choice to act is part of the larger plan and, thus, implies that the whole question is a matter of whether God will be true to Godself.

But post-Shoah this matter is precisely the most troubling. If on the one hand we presume that God is love, then we are confounded by the question of God's being true to God's self. We are confounded because to love in both texts means to offer, to give the son. The object of the offering appears to be clear, that is the election of Abraham has a redemptive direction that requires God's working through humans. Abraham is perceived as an instrument of God's purposes. The place is profoundly mysterious, though. I say profoundly not only because the text says to go where I, that is God, will lead, and the point here must be seen as meaning more than just to the land of Moriah. But this mystery is disturbing to us because now we know with clarity that election can mean Holocaust not in the original understanding of the text but in the nightmare of Auschwitz. This certainty we now have leads us to challenge the whole idea of "Holocaust" as an idea possible to apply to this narrative or any narrative now.

We cannot avoid this tradition however simply because we are horrified by it now. That the gospel text understands the offering in terms of the crucifixion of Jesus and views that as a redemptive act and that this Genesis text views the offering in terms of the moment of God's intervention to free Isaac and substitute the ram is the basis for a tradition that understands love to mean sacrifice. Even on its own terms, the idea is problematic. That God loves the world so much that the elected ones, notably Isaac, are sacrificed for the sake of God's redemption is hard enough to accept on face value. But now we cannot help but see that this election has led to Shoah. Of course, it is not a direct line. Of course, it is not God's intent, which is expressed in this narrative by the theme of intervention. However, it is a link that we cannot blythely ignore.

What this surely means for us is that the test that is set by God of Godself is no longer possible to leave on those terms. If Abraham was quick to challenge God's justice before Sodom, then why not here. The brief reference to Deuteronomy 6 found in the narrative of Jesus' temptation is now not so sure, that we ought not test God. But we realize that the alternative may well mean that we agree with Satan, and that cannot be, not after Auschwitz. Then what? We are left with revising our view of the consequence of love even if it is God's nature. If we must agree with JOB that our vision is too limited to judge God's redemptive activity, even if obedience is still required of us, we must challenge the consequences if that is Auschwitz. We can only do this if now we see that redemption is also ours to produce. That is, if the full impact of the Abraham narrative is realized, that God to be God gives over the plan to human hands. What it means to love is to accept the mutuality of the redemptive plan. If such sacrifice is called for, then Abraham must also intervene. If this is the command, we know what it implies.

Yicchidah (Your Only One)

Seeing the connection we have called election as a love relation produces an intensity and inter-dependence that reinforces the notion of choosing. The other qualifier in the text for Isaac is the command to take the only one. Of course, this command is equally ambiguous as the first since Abraham has more than one son. Thus, the notion of the only one must mean something other than having only one son. Since this point is self-evident, most interpreters have read this qualifier as an additional measure of election -- the only one to whom a promise is given. But there is a promise given to Ishmael as well, so we must say the only one to whom the central role of redemption is given. That is to say, the story marks God's election of a single plan for redemption (to be sure a single plan that is and will become increasingly complex).

This is a claim for exclusivity and remains the ground for such claims in both Judaism and Christianity. Indeed, it is the dividing ground precisely because Jesus is taken to be the only begotten son (John 3:16) and claims to exclusivity tied to redemption have become dividing points. I have saved this discussion to this point in the paper precisely because an exploration of what we have discussed thus far adds new dimensions and questions to this foundation for exclusivity that ultimately challenges normal claims built on such a foundation.

We turn first to the John 3:16 text and its wording, that "whoever believes in him should not perish but have eternal life." On the one hand, this text implies good news, that redemption of this sort is possible. Yet, on the other hand, the stakes are made more serious, we must choose to believe. If we take this text to say this then we have reversed our previous observation and once again made this a human test. God has done God's part and the rest is up to us. Indeed, we could be suggesting that from what we said above about the implications of sacrificial love. But we cannot do this, that is, make all dependent on whether we humans get it right if the result finally is to create boundaries, divisions between those who are right (the only son) and who are wrong (the other sons). Thus, all of what we have said including the present ecumenical necessity of dialogue turns us to some other possible interpretation. What other possibilities are there?

Let us, first, continue to read these texts as a test that God sets before Godself, and if we do so, then we ask what is at stake for God. In this way, we do not make the narrative hinge on human choice even if that choice is invested with power such as we see in both Genesis and John. We have said that humans are not being tested by these choices. Instead there is an implicit test of God imbedded in this qualifier -- the only begotten son. That test appears to call for God's consistency rather than human consistency. The issue is not whether humans are right but whether God is right, essentially true to Godself. At stake is whether God is ambiguous about this choice or whether God would ultimately change God's mind about the choice to redeem. It is precisely this factor that remains for humans a challenge since we cannot see clearly in the course of human living that the evidence shows that God is true to Godself. The old philosophical problem continues to haunt us, if God is good, then, given what we see, God cannot be God.

Of course, Irving Greenberg has laid this challenge in front of Christians rather starkly by suggesting that Shoah has challenged the validity of the central Christian claim, "that God was in Christ reconciling the world to Godself."[4] The fact is, at least from our human perspective, that God is not finished, not done with the test, precisely because God has elected to bring redemption through humans. And the question that penetrates to us from John 3:16 is this question now, what would it take for humans to believe in Jesus as the Christ? This is precisely the precarious nature of the Christian claim after the Shoah.

If John is a true rendering of Genesis, that is provides an insightful and fruitful reading of the *akeda*, then the question we have posed for that text is also the central test rushing forward at us from the *akeda*. What now would it take for God to be believable, for present day Abrahams (or Abrahams of any age for that matter) to trust God. The challenge of the Sodom text, part of that larger context -- isn't it necessary for the Lord of the universe to be just -- now deeply confounds the story of Abraham and Isaac -- is God to be trusted. Is the whole enterprise now in jeopardy because we cannot clearly see that God is or even can be true to Godself, that we can now think that God is just as capable of destruction as of redemption, that God could choose to stand back as a bystander as easily as intervene to provide another kind of sacrifice. How can we not read this narrative in any other way now?

Olah (Burnt Offering)
We have come on a short journey to a profound conclusion, even one that threatens to undo the meaning of the Biblical narratives. It is this set of questions that conspire to set a challenge in front of the two religious traditions that take these texts to be sacred that now do not appear to have answers. Richard Rubenstein has consistently argued that the impact of the Shoah is precisely this demise of the central claims of these two religious visions, each for their separate reasons.[5] Emil Fackenheim has argued that the redemptive voice of God cannot be heard in Auschwitz, and to what extent can we hear that voice after Auschwitz if we are confounded by these questions?[6]

---

[4] Irving Greenberg, "Cloud of Smoke, Pillar of Fire: Judaism, Christianity, and Modernity after the Holocaust," *Auschwitz: Beginning of a New Era?* Eva Fleischner, ed. (New York: KTAV Publishing House, 1974), p. 11ff.

[5] Richard Rubenstein, *After Auschwitz* (New York: MacMillan, 1966), p. 47ff.

[6] Emil Fackenheim, *God's Presence in History* (New York: Harper, 1970), p. 67ff. (References to Fackenheim in the following are to this same text).

Perhaps Fackenheim's solution is a beginning for us in retrieving
this narrative of the *akeda* (we may not in the end be able to do it).
Fackenheim does argue that the commanding voice of God remains in
Auschwitz. In that context, the command can be rendered as a new
commandment -- not to give Hitler any victories. In the same way that the
Genesis text seems to commit God to the human realm as the means of
redemption and we see that notion reinforced in the interpretation offered
through John 3:16, this solution offered by Fackenheim thrusts the question
back on humanity. At least for now, we view redemption as a *tikkun* that can
only arise out of a response to the commanding voice of God. We are not
even sure whether we can speak of redemption as a result of this at all. That
remains the test that God has set for Godself. The ambiguity that was
Abraham's experience remains even more intense. But Fackenheim's
solution means that we now must decide which commands are indeed the
commands of God, which for our generation still means doing that which will
prevent Hitler from achieving any posthumous victories.

Now we can read this narrative only as the command to God and
take the son, the only son, the one that you love. But we cannot assume that
the command must be divine, that is that we are commanded to offer our son
as a burnt offering. Indeed, this command read in that way appalls us now.
We must read this in a different way now since we cannot say that such an
offering is a command from God. The test that is God's cannot any longer
require that of us. There are no more "Holocausts" that can be understood
as a command of God. To continue to say that such offerings are divine
commands is not only a betrayal of the memory of Auschwitz but is now for
us an abomination. This, at least, can be said about the *akeda*.

Chapter 4: The Shoah-Israel Link: Christian Theology Facing Up to the Post-Shoah Era

Between Ben Gurion Airport and Jerusalem is a highway that invites the traveler (especially the first-time visitor) to witness the trees of Israel. Our driver answered my question without hesitation. The forested lands now evident in Israel are the fruit of the labors of the Israelis during the generation of existence of the modern State of Israel. The scenery that greeted my first trip to Israel amazed me. In fact, the contrast between the Jew so often depicted as victim of the Shoah and the Jew who brought trees to the desert was so striking that these two seemed to be unrelated. Only the abstract awareness that comes from study makes one aware that these two Jews are one and the same.

After first impressions, though, and as they fade, a Shoah-Israel link is evident in the ideology and fervor that feeds the modern State of Israel. This connection is evident subtly in the views of many Israelis, both secular and religious. It lies in the mission of the modern Jewish state to insure that the Shoah will never happen again.

Emil Fackenheim, who has done more than most to highlight this mission of the Jewish state, developed his view of Israel from his reflections on the Shoah. In an early work, Fackenheim argued that Jewish tradition hears two different voices from God: the commanding voice and the redeeming voice. While both of these voices remain in normal tradition, Fackenheim cannot imagine that the redeeming voice could be heard at Auschwitz. If the voice of God is heard at all in Auschwitz, it must be the commanding voice. Even so, the extraordinary demands of the death camp meant that the simplest of obligations could become a threat to survival. That is to say, being Jewish not only targeted these people for death according to Hitler's scheme, but also threatened their ability to cope, to survive. In the face of such a twist in horror, Fackenheim argues that the only command that could arise from Auschwitz is the command to survive - not to allow Hitler even a posthumous victory. Indeed, this command deserves a place among the commands of Torah (what Fackenheim has referred to as the 614th commandment).

Fackenheim's vision is captured by this fundamental obligation of Jewish survival but aims at a far more ambitious goal of Jewish mission for *Tikkun Olam* (mending the world).[1] Emil Fackenheim writes, "I saw the trees of the Galilee and was astonished."[2]

A study of the merits of this Jewish theological vision is worthy in its own right. However, even more appropriate for our examination is how Christians can benefit from this vision. An examination of Christian attitudes toward this vision may go a long way in determining how fruitful Jewish-Christian dialogue might be in this post-Auschwitz world. This essay aims to, first, develop the Shoah-Israel link as it is perceived by Emil Fackenheim; second sketch several problematic Christian views of that connection; and, third, show how Christian perspectives might benefit from taking Fackenheim's vision seriously. I conclude by suggesting a few ways that this revised Christian vision might contribute to progress in Jewish-Christian dialogue.

Fackenheim's Vision

In his most recent text, Emil Fackenheim tries to interpret the meaning of a passage in the prophet Ezekiel for post-Auschwitz Judaism. A portion of this text (part of Ezekiel 36) is etched into the wall of the home of the Israeli President. That text coupled with the passage concerning the dry bones that follows in Ezekiel 37 is a classical expression of the hope of Israel even in the midst of exile. Nevertheless, this expression of the traditional view of a resurrection of the dry bones into a people seems, for Fackenheim, to be completely unreasonable following the murder of six million in the Shoah. Even so, Fackenheim can say that the passage has a place in the modern State of Israel even if the classical form of a hoped for resurrection is lost in the ashes of Auschwitz. He writes:

---

[1] Fackenheim's work is clearly of one piece even though it covers a vast terrain. His argument may be traced through various texts, especially the following:

Emil Fackenheim, *God's Presence in History* (New York: Harper and Row, 1970). *To Mend the World* (New York: Schocken, 1982).

2. Emil Fackenheim, "Diaspora and Nation: the Contemporary Situation," *Forum: on the Jewish People, Zionism and Israel,*50 (Winter 1983-84).

"When contradicting this reasonableness, Jews instead opened a new
page in their history – restored a Jewish state – a unique intertwining
of religious faith and secular courage – they resurrected the murdered
hope. The resurrected hope, and it alone, is what remains of Ezekiel's
image of death and resurrection."[3]

Fackenheim's effort to draw Bible and philosophy together in this
latest Shoah theology is remarkable given his own self-understanding: the
philosopher now turned biblical exegete. However, Fackenheim's reading
of Ezekiel suggests that the state of Israel is a symbol of the endurance of
the Jewish people who through that endurance have, themselves,
resurrected the hope expressed by Ezekiel. Those whose tenacity allowed
for survival have given life to dry bones, and God remembers His promise
only afterward. For this reason, the modern state of Israel is necessarily
both religious and secular as both stood side-by-side to produce this
resurrected hope. Fackenheim does not deny the Jewishness of those living
outside the land nor can he deny the Jewishness of the secular Israeli living
in the land. It is the land and the people of the land, though, that
symbolize the endurance and the hope of Judaism in the post-Auschwitz
world. Israel is necessarily, then, a contradiction - a Jewish state that must
count as Jews those who will not identify themselves as religious Jews. But
this contradiction must be the way that we understand Ezekiel, and for that
matter any prophet of hope, today.
        Surely the identity of Israel still finds root in the religious
tradition in the same way that it often has. Still, for Fackenheim, Ezekiel
is both a source for understanding to the religious and a source for political
understanding in the midst of the secular state, symbolically represented in
its place on the wall of the Israeli presidential home. This peculiar mixture
of religious and secular is part and parcel of the Zionist call to the Jewish
world that began the 19th century and eventually made possible the creation
of a Jewish state in the midst of the secular nations. The point is not that
the religious works to eliminate traces of secular apostasy and alien forces,
but that the two serve the same end. At least, Fackenheim's vision of and
for Israel assumes this likelihood and remains consistent from his earliest
works.
        Fackenheim, of course, recognizes that his interpretation of this
Shoah/Israel link has been altered and is less messianic, more apocalyptic

---

3. Emil Fackenheim, *The Jewish Bible After the Holocaust* (Bloomington: Indiana
University Press, 1990), p. 69.

in his words.[4] The point is that any vision for Israel after Auschwitz cannot offer a coherent messianic view but is rather a broken image of stops and starts toward hope that always lies in the tenuous balance between mission and survival. Fackenheim imagined the tenacity necessary simply for the state to survive but he also always envisaged a greater mission than mere survival. His latest words suggest, however, that survival (that this Jewish and democratic state is allowed to work) might be a mission in itself. Still, the vision is the same much as it was for Buber and Herzl. Israel is the Jewish homeland in which all Jews have a right to live in security. Fackenheim's unique extension of that vision is that in Jewish survival both the purposes of God and humankind are served to their fullest.

The Shoah Link

The vision of Jewish development rooted in the land is the consistent theme of Zionism. The point is not nationalism as such even though nationalism (a clearly secular and modern preoccupation) is the form that such a vision must take in the late twentieth century. Nationalism is the peculiarly secular structure that can embrace the pluralism of modern Judaism part of which in Orthodox eyes has itself embraced secularity. Nevertheless, the notion of peoplehood and land is sufficient to understand the vision and is far more compatible with Ezekiel's hope.

The Shoah, however, has put another twist on the mix that shapes Israeli vision. Not only does the nation welcome the refugees of the Shoah (the birth of the nation took on urgency with the influx of survivors and refugees from the Shoah) but the threat to Jewish survival characterized by the Shoah is so grave that the Zionist vision could not help but be re-shaped. In this way, there is an Israel-Shoah link. Again the link is more than just spiritual hope or even political reality but is both and more. The link is the memory that will not fade; this makes Israel a symbol of unity for all Jewry. More than could have been imagined by Herzl or by the young Buber, Israel is home for every Jew everywhere. It is a symbol of the surviving people, and we are naive if we think that this link is only a passing feature of the ongoing Zionist dream. The Shoah has profoundly changed the identity of Israel.

For Fackenheim the problem is in coming to terms with the

---

4. Ibid. Fackenheim, p. 66.

meaning of this twist, finding answers that quiet the soul in its search to explain a reality that so many others cannot begin to grasp. Above all, Israel has been transformed from a haven for the threatened masses in the diaspora to a powerful and self-determining nation state. Israel is a place where trees bloom in the desert and Jewish power has been realized.

Problematic Christian Views of the Shoah-Israel Link

If a Christian vision is to come to terms with this additional dimension that has always been there for the Jew, then the non-Jew must struggle more than Fackenheim with a reality that raises many questions. The Shoah link for Fackenheim has meant the ever evolving nature of Israel, now as powerful state, with a vision that makes Israel unique among the nations. For the non-Jew, the Shoah link has meant another set of images that fit our need for myth and become fodder for our moral judgments but find their roots in fancy, in our world expectation, and not in the reality of the land. There are many versions of our tale, but perhaps two basic storylines.

Non-Jews tend to see that Israel is a product of the Shoah. Israel, in terms of the meaning of some versions, is the gift to the Jews from the West. Our guilt produced modern Israel and continues to blind us to the reality of the moment. This myth is sustained nearly everywhere. So long as we imagine that the myth is true, we will either miss the vision that Fackenheim presents or we will think the vision laughable.[5]   By this version of our story, Israel is a puppet of the West (a little America in the Middle East) or even more sinister Israel is the manipulator who takes advantage of Western guilt. Whichever is the form of this tale, the end result is that Israel as an identifiable, independent people is ignored, even denied.   And Fackenheim is correct, anti-Zionism becomes anti-Judaism when we see the issue on these terms.

At least, as seen through this lens, the Shoah link must be utterly denied. Israel does not owe its existence to either Western guilt or Western political intention.   Israel gained its independence in spite of Western resistance in a war for independence.   The theological/moral ramifications of the unravelling of this fanciful non-Jewish tale is dramatic.   The most

---

5.   Fackenheim clearly sees this tendency toward mythologizing Israel in the Christian community. He has regularly described the directions of our myths as he did in his latest work:

Ibid. Fackenheim, *The Jewish Bible after the Holocaust*, p. 50.

significant result is likely to be the necessity for Christians to come to terms with Israel as a land and a people with independent vision rather than focussing always and unproductively on Christian guilt. Christian guilt may say much about our perspective but very little about the actual character of Israel.

The second version of this gentile tale is the religious Zionism that emanates from Christian apocalyptic fervor. Now this version may actually take on several different seemingly disconnected shapes, but the intent remains consistent. This tale attempts to swallow-up Israel's mission into the "larger" mission of Christianity. Israel's existence corresponds to Christian expectation for the second coming of Christ. On the surface, though thoroughly offensive from the outset, this version seems more prepared to safeguard the independent status of Israel. The necessity for Israel's survival is guaranteed by God. Politically, this Christian response at least implies temporary acceptance. Perhaps, on those terms, this view can be called Zionism, even though the use of the term for this perspective appears dubious to me.

Theologically, this version of the tale is most troubling. By this account, the Shoah link is that ordained by God. Though not expressly made, the connection between God's intent and Hitler's actions is a necessary assumption for this view. One can wonder if even for political expediency the Israeli could long tolerate this obscenity. Surely, the implication is clear for us. This view presumes that Jews are expendable for the sake of God's achieving Christian messianic expectation. There is little sustained love for Israel (and not much commitment to the "land") in this view. Instead, the apparent love for Israel hides a level of hatred that allies itself with centuries of Christian teaching before the Shoah.[6] This new anti-Judaism is one more symptom of what Fackenheim has called the "gentile disease."

The second account given here has shapes that can be purely secular. Many may see Israel as an outpost of American (Western) democracy. Our support for Israel, on these terms, seems little more than a wager on the pragmatic usefulness of Israel for western political purposes. Perhaps there is much of this secular shape of the second tale I have presented in the most recent events in the Persian Gulf. Why are many so surprised, even insulted, that the Israelis were upset at the U.S. for making

---

6. This new form of the teaching of contempt is still like the supercessionism that is so aptly described by many, especially: Jules Isaac, *The Teaching of Contempt: Christian Roots of Anti-Semitism*, (New York: Holt, Rinehart and Winston, 1964).

them targets of scud missiles? Isn't there a lingering feeling that Israel's existence is valid only so long as it serves the interests of the West?

The Shoah-Israel Link
        This latter claim is only a slight diversion from the central point of exploring Christian thinking about Israel as molded by a supposed Israel-Shoah link. Once aware of the mythical versions of this link that penetrate the Christian communities, we can expose and dispel the myths opening up new potential directions of Christian thinking. Several important adjustments can be spotted by exposing the guilt myth so often associated with liberal Christian thinking by Jews (certainly Fackenheim sees this as a typical liberal Christian view).
        We can certainly see how the guilt myth sets up the possibility for a transferal of guilt to Israel. Given the setting of Western guilt for the Shoah as the perceived pre-condition for the existence of Israel, Israel becomes a moral symbol for us as well. We have a great deal at stake in the morality of Israel (that is a morality that suits and benefits us). Since Israel's existence is guaranteed, so many think, by the ongoing guilt from the Shoah, then we see no reason why Israel should not be forever haunted by our guilt, in a sense upholding our best side and overcoming our worst side. Otherwise, why do we so adamantly criticize Israel for actions that are minimal when compared with hundreds of other human rights cases that we systematically ignore? We have too much at stake in Israel and too little at stake in these other places.
        But, we forget too easily that the Shoah constitutes a Christian guilt and not a Jewish guilt. Jews have degrees of feelings, including guilt, that flow out of their Shoah memories; but the guilt of intending and nearly succeeding at the destruction of the Jewish people is not an element of Jewish guilt. This is a Christian burden that we find easily managed if we can pass this guilt on to the Jews, especially the Israelis. Once again, they become scapegoats for us. Once again, we are justified in blaming them. Once again, they are made to be victims, passively accepting our judgments or else receiving our condemnation. And we have a history of living easily with Jews as victims, a history that fed at the very least the twisted road to Auschwitz.
        The only road to escape this pattern is to denounce this new form of the teaching of contempt that grows out of an unrepentant even if guilty moral arrogance. We can escape the trap only by forever breaking this image of the Shoah-Israel link in which Israel is ironically and tragically forced again to hear us compare their actions with Hitler (and what are we

doing otherwise?). The irony of this obscenity is that Hitler and his many collaborators were baptized Christians. The maneuver is to compare Jews with us, to bring Jews down to our level, seen on our terms, where we once again can avoid seeing Jews as Jews.

The second image is equally dangerous even if apparently more supportive. Once exposed, the second myth of the Shoah-Israel link is an unrepentant reiteration of Christian supercessionism. Even if Jews have become used to hearing these things from us, can we continue to tolerate this teaching of contempt from ourselves? Every conflict is seen as a dimension of the good-evil struggle as we define that struggle. Thus, Israel is denied its own unique mission as it is usurped by the "larger" vision of the Christian West. The many shapes of this version of our story continue to feed on the myth of our own superiority in spite of everything that has happened that challenges all notions of Christian and/or Western superiority.

Above all, this belief in the unchallenged apocalyptic vision of the Christian West allows us to ignore, even deny the Shoah. Can we forget that the Christian West and not Israel (and surely not God) was the seedbed for the Nazi genocide? Even if not that,can we ignore that the Christian West almost uniformly failed to respond adequately to the needed rescue of Jews? Can we be so assured that God is on our side or that Western democracies hold the real hope for the future? While we may still believe that democratic freedom is worth striving for (and surely many American Jews have staked their future on this hope), we cannot believe that we have a corner on shaping this hope.

A Return to Fackenheim's Vision

If we can strip away the illusions of our myths about Israel so as to face up to the sinister implications of what remains so typically Christian, then we might be able to return to Fackenheim's vision again with new eyes. Perhaps we can see the way we can join in the hope for Jewish survival that Israel represents in a way that does not allow us to revert to the mythic distortions we are so inclined to hold. Perhaps now we can take seriously the meaning of the land and the people that is Israel. In this land, a people and a vision are engaged in a grand but precarious and confusing journey. The confluence of nationalism and religious hope that makes the everydayness of modern Israel so paradoxical may yet be its greatest strength.

The Land in Fackenheim's Vision

Taking seriously Fackenheim's vision concerning the land is a step both toward guarding against Christian distortions and building a new Christian vision. Fackenheim makes the specific identification of the land an essential part of his view of Israel. Fackenheim does not refrain from linking his new political vision with the religious impulse that also motivates far less flexible views of Jewish claims to the land. The point is that Fackenheim is unwilling to relinquish the Jewishness of the vision and it is that Jewishness that so easily associates with the land that makes the argument strong. Above all, Fackenheim's view, so clearly open to dialogue, is a challenge for Christians since he roots the claim to the land in its religious context.

For Fackenheim, this religious foundation remains a critique of widening assimilation and the tendency toward radical separation. Speaking about a series of "what ifs?" that threatened the survival of the new independent State of Israel Fackenheim says:

> "Had any of these 'what ifs' occurred, there would be no 'Jewish life' worthy of the name; the surviving children of Job − broken by Auschwitz and not mended by Jerusalem, would any be left? − would be an accidental remnant, nothing more; and as for a Jewish 'life with God', this would survive only in those circles, orthodox in the extreme, for which, so long as ten male adults survive to recite the daily prayers, nothing ever happens until the Messiah comes."[7]

The vision, far more complex than I can develop here, at the very least includes this sense that Jewish life can continue only with the attachment to the land that God has promised because only then can the people be challenged by that promise to return to history. Even the landedness bears a physical challenge that must be addressed, a replanting, a commitment to the necessities of earthly living as a people. Thus, the land and not merely the nation (the political entity) is essential to this vision (and Fackenheim dismisses the notion that this return, this mission could be nurtured fully elsewhere like Uganda). It is only in this historical reality that the people can be challenged by their religious roots to take up the mission again. This is truly a Shoah-Israel link in that Fackenheim does not believe that this mission would be possible after Auschwitz

---

7. Ibid. Fackenheim, *The Jewish Bible after the Holocaust*, p. 96.

without the return to the land.

Even as a beginning, Christians must realize this Zionist dimension of Jewish life in our post-Shoah world. Dialogue is impossible if this essential point is denied or dismissed. Too much is invested in this feeling that 'Jewish life' hangs in the balance. Even more though, the point can lead toward both a challenge to the distortions raised earlier herein and become a basis for a new vision. If we take Fackenheim seriously, then we cannot begin to speak about moral issues without taking 'Jewish life' seriously and certainly not such life either apart from land or God. The agenda must begin there and to allow the agenda to begin there is to allow our obligation to Jewish survival to take root. The meaning, if not also the historical possibility, of Israel is not to be found in historical agendas or in Christian guilt but in 'Jewish life' after Auschwitz. Any other beginning point destroys the possibility of talking about moral claims and obligations for anyone. To accept this beginning point is to create the possibility for moral obligation.

Of course, such a view is also to take seriously that there is an independent 'Jewish life with God' from any Christian agenda. We do not have a special claim either to raise our voice on behalf of God or to devise theologies of Israel that serve Christian theologies. Instead, Fackenheim's vision of the land creates the actual possibility for dialogue since Jew and Christian can speak authentically as Jew and Christian without denying the place or the validity of the other (especially not in supercessionist views that swallow up the authenticity of the other). It is our ability to accept this link to landedness that will open the door to new relationships.

But Christians are not used to thinking of religious attachments to land even though Christendom did make that link for a millennium. The notion of God attached to land (at least in terms of promise) is a challenge to our vision of God. Perhaps such challenges are more than mere doors to dialogue and respect. Perhaps Fackenheim's vision of a return to history by a return to earth-boundeness is also a new possibility for Christianity. I do not seek to take up Fackenheim's vision now as a Christian vision. Even so, the attachment to a land is both a lesson in humility (somehow we must struggle with the mundane of the social and political) and in morality, that the good can never be realized as an ideal vision only (even if guaranteed by God, and what is that guarantee now after Auschwitz) but must be worked out in history, in the political arena. If it is not worked out there, if we are not attached to a land, then we might ask whether in our ideal to preserve Christianity we have lost the possibility of 'Christian life.'

The Political/Democratic and Fackenheim's Vision

The great experiment is the democratic experiment that Fackenheim believes is the heritage of a post-Shoah world, also a Shoah-Israel link. Landedness precedes this issue. We cannot talk about a secular state that is also a Jewish state without first accepting Fackenheim's focus on the land. Again, we cannot talk about ideal possibilities or hypothetical cases. Auschwitz has destroyed the last shred of a possibility of doing that. Nevertheless, 'Jewish life' in the modern 'Jewish state' can never again be simply identified as a 'religious state.' Most of the citizens of Israel consider themselves secular (terms such as these are a bit difficult given our Western definitions of the sacred and the secular) even if they are Jewish. Initially that means that being a Jewish state must now necessarily mean being a democratic state. There is no escape from that even if there is always a struggle for the citizens in identifying what that can mean. Still, a recognition of this point as essential to the post-Shoah understanding of Judaism in Israel is the basis for conversation about political privilege, right and obligation. To presume that Israel is not at heart a democratic state is to cut off the possibility of identifying those privileges, rights and obligations.

The secular west may have difficulty in coming to terms with Fackenheim's vision since we generally assume that democracy is the result of free choice. Even if we might be hard pressed to locate a time when any of us actually chose to establish a democracy, we still believe that democracy is our free desire and not a coerced position. Our tradition of inalienable rights comes closest to this notion but still falls short. Democracy, in Fackenheim's view is born out of the necessity of survival and amongst a people who have had little experience with democracy. Survival may be an inalienable right but in the face of Auschwitz survival or rights can never be seen as a political ideal that is always open for negotiation.

Still, the ability to accept Fackenheim's vision is a way to avoid the distortions that plague many non-Jewish views of Israel. The political democracy in Israel today may be financially supported by Western money but it is not justified by that. The justification of Israeli democracy is rooted in the memory of the Shoah and in the basic and everpresent sense of survival in the face of threat so dramatically represented by Auschwitz. Above all, this means that democracy in Israel is not defined nor dictated by the West. And because we often presume too much, our moral challenges of Israel assume that democracy is somehow defined and justified in the same way in Israel as it is the States. The democratic spirit

of Israel arises from the memory of Auschwitz and can only be challenged
to mission out of that memory.

But this is a different memory than ours (we non-Jews). Our
memory is rooted in guilt. The memory that Fackenheim leads us toward
is rooted in survival. Our tendency is to challenge ourselves by guilt (e.g.,
How can anyone who has experienced oppression become the oppressor?).
The Israeli tendency is to challenge each other by the spirit of resistance.
The Israeli memory does not bear the marks of guilt for the Shoah. That is
not the Israeli heritage, the Israel-Shoah link. We do not open up dialogue
by making democratic action and values a matter of guilt. We can open
up dialogue by linking democracy with the memory of survival and the
idea of resistance.

Just how this notion may also be a possibility for a different
Christian vision of the good or of freedom may be worth exploring.
Fackenheim is not particularly interested in setting Christian agendas. He
does, however, speak to an agenda for dialogue. For Fackenheim, the
vision means that the mission of God, if the Jewish people are to continue
to be a people of God, must be rooted in a positive memory. The horror of
Auschwitz has brought doubt about whether such a memory is possible.
But, the point is not whether such a memory can be possible but that such a
memory must be possible. It has always been striking to me that the Israeli
view of the Israel-Shoah link has been predominantly pointed toward the
re-birth of hope in Jerusalem. If that is to mean anything to Jews and
especially to Christians, then Fackenheim believes that we must cling to
the praise given to God's mercy because then we can hope that mercy can
be awakened. We celebrate not only festive occasions but also the disasters
averted all so that mercy is brought forth.[8]

Democracy, even as a Christian vision, can never be rooted only
in individual free choice or in guilt. Even beyond the ways that such an
approach distorts the reality of 'Jewish life in Israel' we must fear the way it
distorts Christian life here and anywhere. Would we not say the same?
That God's mercy is brought forth in our thought and lives not by guilt but
by praise of that mercy? Can we imagine a Christianity that can long
survive such a heavy dose of moral indignation. Morality may be produced
in some ways by raising before ourselves our injustices (how often do we
do it?), but our Christian life is motivated by the mercy (the grace) of God.
Surely, we do not need Fackenheim to remind us of this great truth of our
faith. It is, however, both ironic and hopeful that we are reminded of this

---

8. Ibid. Fackenheim, *The Jewish Bible after the Holocaust*, p. 99.

by Fackenheim.

For Christians, the task of thinking again about Fackenheim's vision is challenged by our ability to come to terms with our own past, with the way that we have sought and jealously guard political power in the name of a fundamentally religious/moral vision. Yet for the sake of maintaining our own integrity in rightly forging the religious and secular in our land(s), we need the ability to engage in dialogue, even partnership, even mutual obligation. For us the Shoah-Israel link may finally be transformed into a teaching of respect, genuine respect, in which we have as an obligation the survival of the people of Israel.[9]

---

9. Of course, Fackenheim long ago suggested this as yet unheeded call for many: Ibid. Emil Fackenheim, *To Mend the World*, p. 285.

Chapter 5: Re-Envisioning Christianity: a New Era in Christian Theological Interpretation of Christian Texts[1]

My work in various dialogues has given me the opportunity to see that theologians tend to incorporate only those materials that seem to be readily adaptable to the dialogue taking place. I have noticed that feminist theologians will often not be sensitive to the dramatic developments in the religion-science dialogue while those in that dialogue are generally unfamiliar with the basic criticisms posed by feminists about both religion and science.[2] I also see that many of the leading thinkers continue to work with theological ideas that fit in their domain of work but do not consider with any seriousness the radical challenges to theology posed by the Shoah and those theologians doing post-Shoah theology.

Once again, I was struck by this phenomenon recently while reading John Polkinghorne's *Belief in God in an Age of Science*.[3] Polkinghorne is surely one of the leading theologians in the science-religion dialogue and this book represents another contribution to the many books he has written trying to develop a new theology in the face of the modern, scientific worldview. He poses one defense for a traditional Christology (a Christian view of the nature of Jesus) as a means for challenging other attempts to adjust such a view in order to fit more comfortably what we know about the world from science. That defense hinges on the necessity to provide an answer to a world full of suffering and evil, a world that produces Auschwitz. In making his defense, Polkinghorne turns to Juergen Moltmann's claim in *The*

---

[1] This essay was presented initially for the Religion, Holocaust and Genocide Group of The American Academy of Religion Annual Meeting, Orlando, November 1998.

[2] I have tried to speak to this issue in:

James Moore, "Cosmology and Theology: The Reemergence of Patriarchy," *Zygon*, (Volume 30: no. 4, December 1995), pp. 613-634.

[3] John Polkinghorne, *Belief in God in an Age of Science*, (New Haven: Yale University Press, 1998).

Crucified God that "Even Auschwitz is taken up into the grief of the Father, the surrender of the Son and the power of the Spirit."[4] The point for Polkinghorne is that Christians need a strong affirmation of the divine and human natures of Christ in order to retain hope in the face of such evil as Auschwitz.

Such arguments are fairly common in theological literature and I was not surprised but rather alerted again to the way that what seems to make sense in one context is outlandish in another. The claim suggests a universalizing of Auschwitz as a symbol of inhumanity against all humans. What is ignored in this claim is the particularity of Auschwitz, the bald fact that this was a killing place where the victims were primarily Jews and the perpetrators primarily, if only nominally Christians. Even more troubling is the implication of the claim that seems to provide comfort and hope for those who believe in a traditional Christology while apparently leaving outside of such hope all the rest including the great majority of the particular victims at Auschwitz. If we stretch even further our analysis, we will surely come to realize that this traditional Christology was one of the important factors that led to the possibility of Auschwitz to begin with.[5] What is hope for some is death for others, a trade-off hardly acceptable in a post-Auschwitz world.

Post-Shoah Theology

This sort of claim made by John Polkinghorne is hardly unique and is possible only if the theologian is not cognizant of the complexity of making theological claims in a post-Shoah world, that is shaping a truly post-Shoah theology. Outside of the participants in dialogue on the question of the Shoah and theologies, we may find defenses of traditional religious views quite the norm and ignorance of the many questions raised by post-Shoah

---

[4] Quoted in ibid., Polkinghorne, p. 44. The more extended context can be found in Juergen Moltmann, *The Crucified God*, (NY: Harper and Row, 1974), and p. 278. In that context, Moltmann takes his cue from Elie Wiesel's imagery in *Night* and suggests that Auschwitz means that God is in Auschwitz and Auschwitz is taken up into God. It is the trinitarian God for Moltmann, however, so Polkinghorne reads him correctly, I think.

[5] cf., Jules Isaac, *The Teaching of Contempt: Christian Roots of Anti-Semitism*, (New York: Holt, Rinehart and Winston, 1964). The classic argument built off of Isaac's study though comes from: Rosemary Radford Ruether, *To Change the World*, (New York: Crossroad, 1983), pp. 31-43.

theologians rather widespread. The problem is not wholly to be found in the ignorance of religious thinkers outside of the dialogue but may also be deeply imbedded in the process of developing post-Shoah theologies as such. The following paper is an initial effort to uncover this problem and move in a different direction that can open up the work of post-Shoah thinking to have a greater impact on the full range of theological thinking.

Polkinghorne's argument reveals interesting clues about the central problem for any post-Shoah theology in that Polkinghorne makes a distinction between ontological and ontic claims.[6] I believe that the distinction he makes blurs the difference and leads him toward a basic theological distortion. For him, ontological claims are those about the way things really are so that to speak of the divinity of Jesus is to speak of something more than just a metaphor but rather to speak of a reality. The difficulty with this line of argument is that it blurs the distinction between the ontological (that which is the foundation of reality) and the ontic (that which we experience as real in the normal sense) because to speak of divinity actually enfleshed in Jesus (a traditional Christian view of the incarnation) is to make the ontological the ontic. This is, of course, the centuries long problem that has faced Christian theologians since the church council accepted the Chalcedonian formula that Jesus is one person with two natures (divine and human). The issue is not just that this talk of two radically different natures wedded together in Jesus is difficult to understand but that the claim means that the ground of all being is reduced to the ontic, to a specific event or set of events in our human experience. If this is more than metaphor but is a claim about reality as Polkinghorne wishes, we have a serious problem.

The problem for dialogue is obvious to most of us in that such a claim at once universalizes the particular Christian belief about Jesus into an ontological reality so that all other efforts to engage in real openness to the other are cancelled because there is always in such a christology a universalizing, supercessionist claim, what Rosemary Ruether spoke of when she said that antisemitism is the left hand of christology.[7] There is no problem for dialogue, even post-Shoah dialogue, to make the ontic claim of the uniqueness of Jesus. In that way, Jesus can be compared with similar claims made by other religious traditions, including Judaism, regarding what is true about our experience of reality as we know it. Shifting the attention to the ontic Jesus has been the central driving force behind my development

[6] Ibid., Polkinghorne, p. 41ff.
[7] Ibid., Ruether, p. 31.

of a midrashic approach to post-Shoah Christian theology[8] in that such an
approach already breaks the universal claim for Jesus by beginning with the
assumption that Jesus is for Christians the oral Torah, that is, by giving
preference for the Torah as the prime source for our understanding of
reality.[9] Of course, what this means is a dramatically different kind of
Christology than the one Polkinghorne wishes to defend.

      The particular theological problem that faces post-Shoah Christian
theology is, however, also symptomatic of a problem in most post-Shoah
theologies as such. For the great majority of thinkers engaged in trying to
shape a post-Shoah theology, the central compelling feature is the
assumption of the uniqueness of the Shoah, but the problem is that such a
claim made as it is leads to a similar blurring of the ontological and the ontic.
The claim is often made with the belief that the Shoah is absolutely unique
in human history, meaning that it becomes a defining event for reality as
such, in this case for the reality of evil. But this means that such theologies
also reduce the ontological to the ontic in a way that universalizes the Shoah
as a supremely defining event and thus reduces all other claims to lesser
subsets of the defining event, the Shoah. The result is that too much
attention is focused on harvesting the unique features of the Shoah for
theological reflection and defending that uniqueness over against all other
possible claims. The end result is not what all of us intend any more than
Polkinghorne intended to reiterate a replacement, supercessionist
christology, that we cannot devise particular ways to respond to
contemporary genocides often because we are committed theologically to
treat them as defined essentially by the particular and unusual features of the
Shoah. Any such theology even if it successfully guards the sanctity of the
Shoah experience of survivors, etc., fails because we have no way to treat
other genocidal activities on their own terms.

Post-Shoah Theology as Post-Modern Theologies

      The second problem may be even more troubling. Post-Shoah
theologies tend to be retrieval theologies even when they are strikingly
different in the content and intent. That is, these theologies are efforts to
make sense of the given religious tradition in the light of the events of the
Shoah. Indeed, I began my efforts with precisely this objective[10] and did so

---

[8] James Moore, *Christian Theology after the Shoah*, (Lanham, MD: University
Press of America, 1993).

[9] Ibid., Moore, p. 29ff.

[10] An thorough description of this approach can also be found in:

because I took seriously the dictum of Irving Greenberg, among many others, that no theological statement can be made after the Shoah unless it could be made in the presence of the burning children.[11] I have expanded that assumption to imply that all post-Shoah theology must be dialogical but I admit that the tendency even in dialogue was to return to the tradition in order to decide if that tradition makes sense, or sense could be made of that tradition, in the light of the events of the Shoah. The focus became "the tradition" and most particularly the scriptural traditions. Even though my objectives were clearly defined from the outset, I cannot deny that my efforts and those of my colleagues have been to retrieve in some fashion the tradition as meaningful even if that meaning were to be a challenge to traditional Christian teaching (thus theology).[12] The approach led to an inter-textual consideration in which certain claims might be made about the genuineness of positions that could then be used to counter positions that are unacceptable in a post-Shoah world even if those latter positions were solidly traditional (like the christology that Polkinghorne seeks so diligently to defend).

The problem again is that this retrieval theology does not account for the radically new context for doing theology that we now face. A theology constructed in dialogue forces the dialogue partners to think about tradition in new ways, ways quite alien to the mindset of those who produced these scriptural texts. We do not account for the fact that the focus shifts from the texts to the dialogue such that the dialogue becomes the authoritative foundation for the new theology. That shift is a vital aspect of the post-Shoah context for theologizing that means more than a shifting away from the authority of tradition, that is a relativizing of tradition as a source for meaning. This shift means that meaning is not resident in texts at all but in action, the action of dialogue.

I have come to realize this fact only after being introduced to a wider range of reflections that can be labeled in general postmodernism. I am especially indebted to the thought of Emanuel Levinas among others who has exposed for me the nature of theological reflection as it is done even in

---

James F. Moore, "Introducing the Dialogue," and "Thinking the Tradition Anew: A New Reading of Genesis 32 and Matthew 26 in Light of the Shoah and Dialogue," *Shofar* (Volume 15: No. 1, Fall 1996), pp. 3-37.

[11] Irving Greenberg, "Cloud of Smoke, Pillar of Fire: Judaism, Christianity, and Modernity after the Holocaust," in Eva Fleischner, ed., *Auschwitz: Beginning of a New Era?* (New York: KTAV Publishing House, 1977), p. 13.

[12] Cf., the special issue of *Shofar*, (Volume 15: No.1, Fall 1996).

the radical context of post-Shoah theologies, the fact that all explanations are rationalizations after the act.[13] That is to say, our efforts to find meaning in texts, even sacred texts, is governed not by the so called meaning carried by the text (as Paul Ricoeur has argued, the text bears a multitude, or surplus of meaning that cannot be contained by a single interpretation which surely always produces a conflict of possible interpretations[14]) but by the events, acts that demand explanation for us. Thus, meaning is really produced within the acting, within the process of acting toward others (even when the other can be an acting toward ourselves).[15]

If theology is always rationalizing after the fact, then we err when we assume that theologies become means for deciding on acts. Indeed, the many studies on rescuing during the Shoah indicate that such rationalizing before the act is rare and often would have led to non-action (which means the rationalizing does not affect the action in either way).[16] The notion that we would or could change peoples actions in the future by changing their theologies (or worldviews or at least confounding their natural tendencies to think in certain ways) does not seem to hold. Meaning is not resident in texts, then, but is itself a process that emerges only when we act (as Levinas says as we act for the other).

This insight has led me to see that post-Shoah theologies must make this next step that moves us away from any reconstructing of worldviews toward theologies rooted in ethics. That is, all post-Shoah theology must be postmodern theology in which both of the problems I have addressed are answered with a radically new approach. All religious narratives turned toward theologies have this universalizing tendency that creates barriers for dialogue. Certainly Christianity is a prime example. If we assume a postmodern position however, we accept that there is no grand narrative of meaning within which all else is defined. Thus, the retrieving of a christology as a unique feature of Christianity (even in the vein of Roy

---

[13] Emanuel Levinas, *Totality and Infinity: An Essay on Exteriority*, (Pittsburgh: Duquesne Univ. Press, 1969).

[14] Ricoeur has spent a lifetime detailing his interpretation theory, but two resources quite helpful in grasping the points related here are:

Paul Ricoeur, *The Conflict of Interpretations* (Evanston: Northwestern University Press, 1974), and

Paul Ricoeur, *Interpretation Theory* (Fort Worth: Texas Christian University Press, 1976).

[15] Ibid., Levinas, p 119.

[16] Cf., Samuel and Pearl Oliner, *The Altruistic Personality*, (NY: The Free Press, 1988). They also give a thorough bibliography of other important work on rescue.

Eckardt who argues that only a crucified Jesus can do[17]) becomes a non-question except as one candidate among many for providing meaning for our experience. The focus is on an unfolding narrative not on maintaining the status of a received narrative (thus a reshuffling of the way that post-Shoah theology handles the Shoah narratives). And if we assume a postmodern theology, then we accept that meaning is emerging in the ways we act for the other (again, even when that acting is toward ourselves as the other).

Moving Toward a Postmodern, Post-Shoah Theology

I was struck again by two examples of recent efforts at shaping a post-Shoah theology, one Christian and one Jewish. I choose these two because both are moving in the direction I am suggesting but both, in the end, fall back into one or both of the two problems I have set forth here. Darrell Fasching's effort in *Narrative Theology after Auschwitz*[18] is a prime example for me since he does in his book much of what I have tried to do in my work. I find a compatriot in him and see so clearly in his work what doing post-Shoah theology in this way means. He is clear about the role of theology in a post-Shoah world as both constructing a new narrative and leading us more and more toward a universal ethic of respect.[19] Indeed, his epilogue follows the pattern of a midrashic theology much like I have tried to do. He turns to Jacob as a narrative source for shaping a post-Shoah Christian theology. He appeals to Irving Greenberg as a challenge to be heeded for critiquing Christian theologies. He concludes by applying the insight of the Genesis text about Jacob to the contemporary conflicts in the Middle East. His argument is striking in that he aims the theology toward Christians, disowning a critique of Israelis, a fascinating effort to open the door for dialogue by making the Christian view one among many.

But Fasching's appeal to the text of Genesis inevitably leads to the conclusion that meaning is found in the text and post-Shoah theology aims to bring genuine meanings of traditional texts to bear on contemporary conflicts. Instead of seeing that the multiplicity of meanings carried by texts

---

[17] A. Roy Eckardt and Alice Eckardt, *Long Night's Journey into Day* (Detroit: Wayne State University, 1982), pp. 125ff.

[18] Darrell Fasching, *Narrative Theology After Auschwitz*, (Mpls.: Fortress Press, 1992).

[19] Ibid., Fasching, p. 192ff.

leads us to ambiguity, Fasching sees that the unique character of Auschwitz
forces us to see a meaning that must be the central defining ethic for
Christians in a post-Shoah world (the ethic of respect for the stranger). In
fact, there is much to commend in this argument and his position which calls
for Christians (mostly Palestinians I assume) to take on this ethic is
interesting. The problem is that the text is shaped by a context different from
both that of Auschwitz and the present Middle East conflicts. Imposing the
meaning of the text on this particular conflict resolution is to impose a
universal meaning from the text (even if the aim is one of persuasion) rather
than to see that the dialogue between Israelis and Palestinians is the focus of
meaning, a meaning which must emerge from that dialogue and not from
meanings resident in texts. I am fascinated by Fasching's appeal finally that
it is time for all religions (cultures) to assume this ethic of respect for the
stranger, but that only shows the power of this universalizing tendency found
in efforts to retrieve meaning in texts.

     Indeed, Fasching's efforts are exemplary and represent the best of
what we see in post-Shoah theological thinking. Nevertheless, a post-Shoah
theology needs to make the next step toward a recognition that meanings
emerge in the context of acting (even dialoguing) for the other. Meanings
are in process and the meanings of the text may not be retrievable as
meanings for the future or even the present. The claim that a narrative
tradition can provide guidance for all religions must be made with caution
since we realize more and more that there is no grand narrative that can
function in that way and surely the narratives of the Hebrew scriptures as
pregnant with meaning as they are, are also subject to the radical suspicion
that the Shoah itself thrust itself upon them.

     Equally interesting is Peter Haas' *Morality after Auschwitz*[20] for
Peter has developed an approach to ethics that moves toward the sort of
effort that I am suggesting (an emerging ethic in the context of acting). The
text concludes with a quotation from Albert Speer that emphasizes the
transient nature of ideology in Nazi Germany. The developments toward a
final solution produced actions that were not part of original conceptions and
ideologies, at least for most in the Nazi camp. That is, the Nazi ethic was an
emergent ethic that was only partially dependent on an ideology that was well
set in the 1920's. The ideology (rationalization for action) was itself an
emergent reality so that with each new development we can see a shift in
rationalization and thus ideology. Haas' book is written in such a way so as

---

[20] Peter Haas, *Morality After Auschwitz*, (Philadelphia: Fortress Press, 1988).

to emphasize this fact. Thus, we see that for Peter Haas the lesson most evident that we learn from the Shoah is that an ethic must and probably always does emerge in the context of particular acts and events. Thus, a post-Shoah morality must incorporate this recognition that ethics is an emergent reality and not effective if strictly shaped by tradition or ideology.

The issue for Haas and for me, though, must be why this is a lesson we necessarily must learn from the Shoah. There is no question that the Shoah is a unique historical event that draws together features that can be found at various times throughout Western history, at least. Perhaps we can argue that the Shoah is a particularly transparent event that lets us see things that we would otherwise miss. Even so, I wonder about the validity of such claims that assume that a particular focus on the Shoah teaches us lessons that are otherwise not available to us. Assuming that pose leads us to two rather troubling tendencies. First, we assume that little or nothing is learned from the past, only waiting for the Shoah to be brought home. By assuming that the Shoah is the defining event in history we assume a posture that this history of humankind is a gradual slippery slope sliding downward toward the depravity of Auschwitz which finally wakes us up to our potential evil. Any broader historical reading of genocide would, however, lead us to see that human brutality was at least as devastating in the past if not more so and that maybe humanity has learned some of these lessons along the way. We see that it is all too easy to see our event as the defining one and to let that event shape our reading of human history, human nature, and ethics.

Second, the tendency is to assume that the Shoah is a universally defining event so that after Auschwitz we still return to those events as defining for us. This makes for a grand success for our courses on the Shoah, but we may be better served by placing the Shoah into the larger context of human violence that is still being defined by many other examples from which lessons can be learned. This does not diminish the importance of the Shoah but rather opens up even more our acceptance of the emergent nature of reality and morality, which is after all the real intent that Haas brings to his book.

Thus, I urge us to make the next step forward that means the move toward seeing that any post-Shoah theology must be a theology constructed in dialogue (an ever-expanding dialogue preferably) with the focus on dialogue and not on received traditions. What we have learned is that the demands of real dialogue do lead us toward radically new positions but have the potential even more to do this if we abandon the necessity for finding meaning in the texts of our traditions. Secondly, we need to make the move forward to see that the question of uniqueness is misplaced in a post-Shoah theology since this leads us to continue to put forward the Shoah as the defining event (in the same way that Polkinghorne needs to defend classical Christian christology as the defining -- ontological-- human event) under which all else must be subsumed. There is still in us a need to refuse all such universalizing tendencies, but even more to recognize that meaning is an emerging reality and emerges in the context of acting and not in rationalizing and ideologies (not even in noble theological ethics) which are, in fact, rationalizations after the act. Our attention moves away from constructing theologies toward narrating this emerging ethic, which I believe is the desire of both Haas and Fasching and for that matter many if not most of those trying to do post-Shoah theology.

A Postscript -- Religionless Theology

One of the more fascinating concepts that did emerge from the context of the Shoah was Dietrich Bonhoeffer's idea of religionless Christianity.[21] Interpreters have delighted in trying to understand what Bonhoeffer meant. My fascination is not so much based on what Bonhoeffer meant but by the possibility of the idea in the context of a postmodern, post-Shoah theology. What does seem to me to be the case is that when we follow the path described in this paper, we move more and more toward a "religionless" theology.[22] If we are not at the task of retrieving a tradition as such, we are not trying to defend or continue that tradition into the future. The focus is not only moving away from the retaining of a tradition by giving it renewed meaning, but rather away from the maintaining of Christianity as a unique religious position as such. It is a searching for something quite new

---

[21] Dietrich Bonhoeffer, *Letters and Papers From Prison*, (NY: Macmillan, 1967), p. 140ff.

Bonhoeffer spoke of this idea at various places in the letters and links it to a notion both of Christianity continuing without taking the form of religion and without the working hypothesis of God. These ideas are, of course, never fully developed and they imply a link to the tradition even if that link is perceived in a radically new way. It is this sense of a radically new link that I propose the argument that follows. His ideas, however, are akin to what might be found in various contemporary thinkers such as Don Cupitt, Gordon Kaufman, Raimon Panikkar, and David Tracy as presented in their articles in a recent issue of *Cross Currents* (Volume 50: nos. 1-2, Spring/Summer 2000), pp. 56-67, 103-111, 185-195, 240-247.

[22] This idea really does not mean a demise of religion as source but a position closer to that of John Caputo and, with that, to Jacques Derrida in his more recent writing on religion. Cf., John D. Caputo, *The Prayers and Tears of Jacques Derrida: Religion without Religion* (Bloomington, Indiana University Press, 1997).

and different. I am still challenged by my own dictum that any post-Shoah theology is obligated to support the survival of and thriving of Jews and Judaism (following Emil Fackenheim's famous commandment).[23] But now I see that my aim is not a theological one at all as if it were necessary for Christians to give theological defense for Jewish tradition (whatever form of Judaism we may mean). Instead, I am arguing for an ethical principle that simply is one extension of the basic ethical principle of respect for all others as others. What a postmodern theology does, however, is to refuse to ground that ethic in Christianity for the survival of Christianity as such is not necessary for such an ethic. Indeed, the future may lead us toward something quite other than Christianity. Even so, this ethical principle will likely continue to give us good reason to talk about texts and meanings in texts so as to challenge the idea that there is such a thing as a Christian reading, or meaning, or reality. Our hope may lie in the emerging realization of this reality and the emerging reality that does not need to preserve religious traditions as rationalizations for action.

---

[23] See, Moore, *Christian Theology after the Shoah*, p. 132. Also, this position connects with the important concept developed in:

Emil Fackenheim, *God's Presence in History*, (NY: Harper and Row, 1970), p. 84.

Chapter 6: Recovering the European Perspective on Post-Holocaust Theology

There are four claims that I will make in this chapter. First, I believe that American post-Shoah theology can and is making a major paradigm shift as American theologians take more seriously the contributions of European thinkers on the Shoah. My own development is but one example of this shift and the following paper offers my narrative as an example of this change in thinking. Second, I believe that the shift in thinking that is taking place can be understood especially by seeing the range of positions in post-Shoah theology through the lenses of postmodern thought, especially as it is observed in Europe. I offer the comparison of the work of Paul Ricoeur and Emmanuel Levinas as an illustration of the options within postmodern thinking that will illuminate the direction of the paradigm shift I am suggesting. Third, I further contend that a consideration of the difference between Jewish and Christian responses, especially in Europe can be a critical guide for understanding the differences between different postmodern positions, like that of Ricoeur or Levinas or even like the thought of Emil Fackenheim. Finally, I argue that the central nature of this paradigm shift in American post-Shoah theology is a move away from a focus on a retrieval of religious narratives after the Shoah toward an emphasis on ethics as central. What this means, finally, is a deconstruction of religious identity in favor of a view of emerging identity that takes shape only in interactions between moral agents within the moment of "acting for the other" as Levinas puts it.

My Narrative For Example

Ten years ago I delivered a paper at an international Holocaust conference in Oxford which was a beginning to a realization that any theology done now must be a post-Shoah theology.[1] That realization meant

---

[1] James Moore, "The Holocaust and Christian Theology: A Spectrum of Views on the Crucifixion and the Resurrection in the Light of the Holocaust," in

two things: (1) that the Shoah now becomes an integral part of any religious narrative since I was convinced that the Shoah represents a primary and absolute challenge to religious claims, and (2) that theology done now cannot really provide answers to the experiences of the Shoah (as varied and complicated as those narratives are) since there are no such explanations that can account for the motivations of either the perpetrators or the victims. Thus, theologies that are fashioned now with this realization cannot be the same as theologies that were shaped before the Shoah and all such pre-Shoah theologies are now obsolete in critical ways. Those insights were put into practice and shaped more fully in my subsequent work.[2]

The approach that emerged from these assumptions I labeled a midrashic approach both because the style of midrash set certain rules for interpretation that became cornerstones of post-Shoah theology for me and because theologies must now be theologies in dialogue. Thus, the adoption of the language of midrash was a self-conscious effort to make theology dialogical even if all the partners in dialogue are not actually present in the shaping of a theology. This midrashic approach meant, of course, that any post-Shoah theology begins with a return to scripture in order to uncover readings of scripture that can no longer be valid given the exigency of a post-Shoah way of thinking. This initial effort was designed not to produce a new narrative but to challenge any final interpretation and to establish rules for reading scripture that would guard against any notion of a single meaning for any text. The fundamental principles that guided this work were the recognition of the plurality of possible meanings for any text and the ambiguity of all scripture that cannot give precedence to any of these possible interpretations.[3]   In this line of thinking the only possible conclusions would be the exclusion of some interpretations on the basis of a post-Shoah critique of the "teaching of contempt" in the history of Christian theology.[4]

Remembering for the Future, Franklin Littell and Yehuda Bauer, ed., (Oxford: Pergamon Press, 1988), vol. I, pp. 844-857.

[2] James Moore, Christian Theology after the Shoah (Lanham, MD: University Press of America, 1993).

[3] David Tracy, Plurality and Ambiguity (New York: Harper and Row, 1987).

[4] Jules Isaac, The Teaching of Contempt (New York: Holt, Rinehart and Winston, 1964).

I realize now, a decade later, that even this exercise has the potential for leading to an attempt at retrieval of these texts. To claim the plurality of possible meanings and the ambiguity produced by that does allow for the assumption that the texts still have the potential for producing meaning and that among the variety of options for understanding these texts that emerged prior to the Shoah, some might be counted as legitimate for a post-Shoah theology. I admit that my approach does lean in this direction partly because I was influenced in my thinking by the writing of Paul Ricoeur and with the sense that the narratives always contain a surplus of meaning that makes the project of retrieval of texts worthwhile even within the harsh critique of the Shoah.[5] At the very least, texts became in this thinking a source for rules for reading that eliminate any reading of texts that reinforce the teaching of contempt and at best produce a teaching of respect.[6] This was clearly a goal of my work and this goal was fashioned by my interaction with important thinkers in the post-Shoah dialogue in the States, principally Irving Greenberg.[7] What is most surprising for me now is the influence of Ricoeur whose ideas were shaped far more by the battles over postmodern thinking within intellectual circles in Paris, that is, in the European, post-Shoah world than by American post-Shoah theology.[8]

As I think now about this process of thinking that led to the midrashic approach, I realize even more that my thinking was also profoundly influenced by two European thinkers who delivered papers at the very same conference in Oxford a decade ago. It seemed to me then that thinking on the continent was strikingly different than that in the States and

---

[5] Paul Ricoeur, *Interpretation Theory* (Fort Worth: Texas Christian University Press, 1976).

[6] cf., Clark Williamson, *When Jews and Christians Meet* (St. Louis, CBP Press, 1988).

[7] Irving Greenberg, "Cloud of Smoke, Pillar of Fire..." in *Auschwitz: Beginning of a New Era?*, Eva Fleischner, ed. (New York: KTAV, 1977).

[8] As a term, the notion of a postmodern era is widely debated and while the term is used in the 1930's, there is reason to believe that the main themes of postmodern thought were shaped by a circle of thinkers which included both Ricoeur and Levinas as well as Derrida and Foucault and Sartre and Demans in Paris in the 1950's and 60's. cf., Barry Smart, *Postmodernity* (London: Routledge, 1993).

that any post-Shoah theology cannot be developed without serious integration of European thinkers. In this early stage of my own thought development. Hyam Maccoby set for us a challenge that ran to the very core of doing theology itself.[9] He simply said that if Christians were ready to do away with the narratives of the crucifixion and resurrection, then Christian theology would be far more acceptable. Of course, the suggestion was met with dismay by many since such a move would remove the uniquely Christian core to the Christian scriptures. What would be left would be essentially the Jewish teachings and lifestyle of Jesus. Of course, this claim was readily dismissed by most as unthinkable and for Maccoby simply a sign that real dialogue would remain fruitless. I now see that his challenge led me to my work on these narratives as the central focus of my book on post-Shoah Christian theology. Even so, I now see much more than even then in Maccoby's challenge, that which has led me to explore the major distinctions between European and American thinking on the Shoah.

Jacobus Schooneveld set the other parameter to my research by posing the notion that in the gospel of John Jesus is portrayed as the oral Torah.[10] What this meant for my work was a profound shift in approach that may be my most important contribution to the dialogue to this point, that all Christian scripture is an interpretation of Torah and must be re-united to the specific texts of Torah in midrashic fashion in order to make any sense. Thus, Schooneveld gave me another and very central tool for judgment on the possible meanings of any Christian text. I understood then that such a move would ultimately strip Christianity of any unique status and place Christian thinking on Torah into a direct and equal conversation with Rabbinic Judaism. Indeed, the notion leads to a dismissal of Christianity as it developed over the millennia in favor of a radically new Christianity of a post-Shoah world. Such a break in history which I now brought to all reflection on Christian narratives represents something like the idea of "tremendum" as presented by Arthur Cohen and takes with radical seriousness the idea presented by Johannes Metz that no theology is valid in

---

[9] Hyam Maccoby, "Antisemitism and the Christian Myth," in *Remembering for the Future*, Franklin Littell and Yehuda Bauer, ed. (Oxford: Pergamon Press, 1988), vol.I, pp. 836-843.

[10] Jacobus Schooneveld, "Torah in the Flesh," in *Remembering for the Future*, Franklin Littell and Yehuda Bauer, ed. (Oxford: Pergamon Press, 1988), vol. I, pp. 867-878.

a post-Shoah world that does not take seriously the challenge of the Shoah.[11] I believe that I have given the thought of these thinkers a twist which is my own and not so much the intent of the thinkers themselves. Even so, it is clear that my thinking was profoundly influenced by an exposure to European post-Shoah thinking that tempered and changed the approach already long developed by American theologians.

My return to the roots of my own post-Shoah theology has led me once again to a realization that European thinkers have an important if not central role in a full development of American post-Shoah theology and has led me back to these critical ideas that shaped my own thinking. Thus, my own narrative leads ultimately to my first assertion that a full integration of European thought into American post-Shoah theology can and will lead to a dramatic paradigm shift in American post-Shoah thought. The opportunity to re-examine the question what if anything is distinctive about European thought on the Shoah has now produced surprising new questions and directions for research that I admit are only just taking shape. Thus, I present these reflections as barely beginning insights that nevertheless at this point of awareness seem of great significance. I was led to see even more clearly these new insights when I returned to Ricoeur, in particular to Ricoeur's analysis of Emmanuel Levinas. In Ricoeur's analysis I saw not only that European thinkers bring dramatically new insight but that there may be significance as well in sorting through the differences between Christian and Jewish thinkers. Above all, I discovered even more than I had before that the question of a post-Shoah theology was indeed the question of postmodernism and brought into focus the central questions and debates that have taken place primarily in Europe on the nature of postmodernism and postmodern thought. That this debate is much more fundamentally European than American may be a critical factor in the very real differences between American and European post-Shoah thinking. Even more, I believe that the debate in Europe on postmodern reality and thinking may very well be better understood as essentially a debate over the impact of the Shoah which means that thinkers with Jewish intellectual roots will most certainly differ from those with Christian intellectual roots. In addition, if the issue is really a post-Shoah issue as I understood a decade ago but now can apply to this new set of questions, then it is all the more likely that the European experience

---

[11] Arthur A. Cohen, *The Tremendum* (New York: Crossroad, 1981).
and
Johann Baptist Metz, *The Emerging Church* (New York: Crossroad, 1986), pp. 20ff.

leading to European thought is critical for any American post-Shoah theology. The difference is that the debate over postmodern reality now becomes even more a critical source for American post-Shoah theology than it has thus far.

Ricoeur on Levinas

I do not wish to reproduce Ricoeur's analysis of Levinas which after all appeared first in 1989.[12] The point is neither to accept a position like that of Levinas or of Ricoeur but to recognize questions that emerge if we look again at Ricoeur's analysis in light of the claim that to be postmodern is fundamentally tied up with being post-Shoah at least in the European context. Above all, my attention is captured by Ricoeur's decision to think about Levinas in the context of the notion of testimony even though, by Ricoeur's admission the notion appears to be marginal to Levinas' thought. I ask, why this decision? What seems to be crucial is that for Ricoeur testimony requires a self, an identity that is rooted in a past, in an established narrative and Levinas speaks about a self that is unsaid, a self that is no longer rooted in this way. What I found was that Ricoeur and Levinas represent poles within this postmodern debate on the validity of narratives as foundations for moral responsibility and ethical action. That is, this comparison of Ricoeur and Levinas is one example of my second point, that the possible shift in American post-Shoah theology can best be understood by observing postmodern thought, especially as it can be seen in the European context.

That is, Levinas no longer presumes a narrative ontology for any sense of the self. There is no structure out of which responsibility emerges and thus no ready made identity that gives shape (that is, rationale) to action. I believe that Levinas reaches this conclusion primarily because the events of the Shoah, in particular, have shown the futility of modernity and have made efforts to give ideological rationale for ethical action invalid. Thus, Levinas' rejection of ontology is a rejection of all narratives as motivation for action as ways of understanding the self. This perception of the "freed self" that Ricoeur finds in Levinas is not a perception that is lost in despair. For Levinas there is a happy movement from ontology to ethics as the focus that realizes a complete break from ontology, certainly a break from Heidegger and the whole existentialist-phenomenological school of thought

---

[12] Paul Ricoeur, *Figuring the Sacred* (Minneapolis: Fortress Press, 1995).

represented by Heidegger. For Levinas, ethics emerges as primary and the self becomes a self only in acting for the other.

One notices immediately in Levinas the postmodern theme of the breaking of narrative so that identity is no longer to be found in the fashioning of a narrative or a retrieval of a narrative or a development of a new narrative. Identity is located in the unsaid, the actions, the externality of acting. Ricoeur is not satisfied since he believes that such a move assumes a self that lurks in the shadow of acting. Thus, in these two thinkers we find two poles in postmodern thought. Ricoeur believes that we can retrieve meaning in narratives and thus ground the self in the world created by the narrative while Levinas is suspicious of any ontology, even the world created by narratives. For Ricoeur, then, the religious narratives become a source for understanding action and morality while for Levinas they can only be after the fact rationalizations that say nothing about real selves acting as moral agents. The only way to move beyond narrative is to recognize the testimony of the unsaid, that is of pure action in which and only in which the self can emerge. For Levinas this means that the self can become, can emerge only in the action "for-the-other." For Ricoeur, the self can emerge only if a self, that is a self formed by narrative is motivated to act for the other.

My question is why the difference and can we see some beginnings of an answer by thinking about this analysis in light of the insight that postmodern means to a great extent post-Shoah. I think that it is only in the light of this connection that the debate between Ricoeur and Levinas can be understood and this tool of analysis that I am applying also leads us to my third point, that in recognizing the difference between Jewish and Christian responses to the Shoah we can understand more fully the reasons for the difference between Ricoeur and Levinas. What is remarkable is that Ricoeur does not account for this factor in his analysis treating Levinas only on philosophical terms and not recognizing either the importance of the Shoah as a shaping factor or of Levinas' Jewish heritage as important for understanding Levinas' philosophical thought.

It appears to me that the debate between Levinas and Ricoeur becomes one aspect of the struggle for identity, especially in the European context, after the Shoah. I can still remember sitting with Ricoeur in 1980 as he struggled to make sense of Heidegger in a seminar at the University of Chicago. I believe now that he continues to struggle since he realizes that Heidegger's ontological approach cannot help us retrieve even in a broken way the narratives that help construct our identities, even the identity of the self. Thus Ricoeur also rejects Heidegger's ontology and argues for what he calls a hermeneutic of suspicion. On the one hand, this difference that has led Ricoeur constantly back to the questions of self and narrative as a way of thinking about action and led Levinas to abandon such efforts is part of a long philosophical struggle with the phenomenological school of thought. Even so, Ricoeur's desire to retrieve the meanings in narratives, particularly religious narratives, and Levinas' desire to break free completely from narratives to a radical postmodern ethic may be a difference understood more fully by recognizing that Ricoeur sees the Shoah as a culmination of a narrative perpetrated on the other, on the Jew, by Christian Europe and Levinas approaches the same with the awareness that this was an event perpetrated on his own people.[1]

That Ricoeur does not give any account of this difference in thinking about the Shoah leaves the difference as only a philosophical one rather than as a difference in identity as such, that is to be one who inherits the experience of the perpetrator rather than one who inherits the experience of the victim. I will leave this only as a hunch for now recognizing that my hunch needs much more work to determine if there is any validity in my claim; however I am clearly not the first to sense the importance of this factor of Jewish identity since Zygmunt Bauman argued in 1990 that Jewishness does play a significant role in shaping the experience and interpretation of modernity and of the Shoah. Thus, a sociological analysis that accounts for this factor is very likely an important tool for understanding differences between thinkers like Ricoeur and Levinas.

I would push the point even further by suggesting that for both Ricoeur and Levinas the matter of identity after the Shoah means a real break with the institutions of religion that were for centuries the main carriers of the narrative traditions. This break would be different for the perpetrator and the victim but the break is real nevertheless. In this way, I believe that European thinkers see the issue of identity in a very

---

[1] Zygmunt Bauman captured what I am trying to say rather well in an interview which was included in his book *Intimations of Postmodernity* (p. 226) where he says:
Well, there were three stages in which Jewishness played some role in my life...The second stage was Janina's [Bauman] Holocaust book [1986]. It may seem really bizarre, but I did understand for the first time what the Holocaust meant when I read her book. I knew that there was a Holocaust -- everybody knew that there was a Holocaust -- but it was an event 'over there', somewhere else. As I said in the Preface to my Holocaust book, I saw the Holocaust as a picture on the wall, and then, suddenly, I saw it as a window, through which you can see other things."
Zygmunt Bauman, *Intimations of Postmodernity* (London: Routledge, 1992).

different light than do American thinkers and with this we have a
significant difference in the way that Europeans and Americans have
approached post-Shoah thinking. This difference is especially obvious
in Jewish circles since the institutions of European Jewry were
decimated by the Shoah. This means that Jewish thinkers in Europe are
far more likely to emerge in the academy and associate with the
academy while Jewish thinkers in the States will generally be found
among both rabbis serving synagogues as well as academics. Even if it
is less the case for Christian thinkers in Europe, I believe we have not
thought enough about how Christians in the States are radically
different in that they can still connect with the institutions of the
churches in ways far more obvious than can their counterparts in
Europe. This factor must become more obvious in any development of
American post-Shoah theology than has happened thus far.

Fackenheim for Example

        The essay by Ricoeur only opens the doors for further
exploration of the claims I am making. I am led back to the two figures
that so shaped my thinking just a decade ago now with this new set of
questions emerging as a way of understanding what Maccoby and
Schooneveld were saying at that conference in Oxford. To be sure,
Maccoby was suggesting a radical departure for Christian theology that
would mean both a new relationship between Christians and Jews as
well as a strong post-Shoah critique of Christian narratives for any
post-Shoah theology. But what if we saw Maccoby's position now
further enlightened by this set of questions I found present in Ricoeur's
analysis of Levinas? What if Maccoby's challenge were to be seen as a
postmodern challenge in the same vein as Levinas' rejection of
ontology and move to an ethic in action? Indeed, it now seems
appropriate to read Maccoby in this way since his focus was on liturgy
and the relation between liturgy and actions (not so much on worldview
but on immediate actions that arise from liturgy). The point for
Maccoby may well have been precisely what is my fourth claim that
American Christian theology after the Shoah can have legitimacy only
if it moves away from ontology, away from worldview building,
toward a focus on action, in this vein of action "for-the-other."
Maccoby's point would not have been so much a focus on the removing
of a set of narratives or a retrieval of those narratives (the passion
narratives) for any purpose, even for liturgy, but rather a re-direction of
theology, itself, that is, a paradigm shift. To do that would require an
abandoning of ontology, of narrative building. Indeed, this may require

abandoning the unique identity of being a Christian for the sake of an emerging ethic, an ethic that emerges in acting for the other as Levinas argues. This suggestion is even more radical than many thought was Maccoby's point at the time in that the issue is not a refashioned Christianity at all but rather a break with being Christian as having any real significance in a post-Shoah world. In such a world, only the self that is unsaid, the self that emerges in action for the other is genuine.

If the argument makes sense thus far, we can now begin to identify exactly what this new paradigm for American post-Shoah theology would involve. First, can we construct theologies that deconstruct Christian identity, especially the ontological necessities that make the narratives of separate Christian identity important to us, more important even than the ethic of action for the other? My odyssey over the last decade has gradually moved in this direction realizing all along that this is the insight that needs to be realized in post-Shoah theology, but I believe I was delayed in this move because I chose to read the whole discussion through Ricoeur's notions of narrative and retrieval and I chose to follow the direction of a midrashic approach that was shaped not by the European thought of Maccoby or Levinas but by that of Ricoeur, especially as that has been developed by David Tracy.[2] My case is only one example but may be representative of most of American post-Shoah theology. Only a few of those involved with post-Shoah theological thinking in America have incorporated European postmodern thought into their theologies while most are still working to retrieve in some re-visioned form some kind of unique Christian theology adequate to respond to the challenges of the Shoah.

I can take this analysis a step further by looking again at the insight of Jacobus Schooneveld. The idea that Jesus is the oral Torah does hold within it the radical possibility of a deconstructing of Christian identity which collapses all Christian narrative into an interpretation of Torah. The immediate implication of that move is to put Christian thought on the same plane as all forms of Rabbinic thought, thus reinforcing my decision to fashion a midrashic approach. Even my sense of developing rules for reading was a way of deconstructing tradition and breaking of narrative. But the move lacks the next step that only a view from Levinas can provide. For Levinas, the break with ontology means that the context for the emerging self is the moment of acting for the other. In that sense, the self always

---

[2] David Tracy, *The Analogical Imagination* (New York: Crossroad, 1981).

emerges before the narrative, before anything is said. To deconstruct Christian narrative in such a way so as to place it into the tradition of oral Torah stills suggests that there is a narrative place for identity, that is my identity as self places me as one example of a long line of others who have been part of a tradition.. The radical form of Levinas' move would see in oral Torah the embodiment of the postmodern principle that Levinas iterates, the breaking of narrative for the sake of an ethic that is emerging in acting for the other. Indeed, this is what Torah is in the tradition of oral Torah, that is in the actual midrashic tradition since there is no narrative before the acting. The acting produces the possibility of narrative and since that is the case, the narrative is always open-ended, always constructed after the acting and is always potentially radically new with each new emerging self. The only problem with the history of this tradition of oral Torah is that it has led to an orthodoxy, rather an orthopraxy, in the formation of the Talmud and the Halachic tradition. That tradition is precisely what is challenged in the Shoah and what while remaining in remnant form in the thought of Levinas and others is finally broken by a new reality made urgently necessary by the Shoah. To follow the tradition just did not work as a way of responding to the Shoah.

This insight can be drawn out further by looking at another post-Shoah European thinker, Emil Fackenheim. That Fackenheim became one of the most significant contributors to Israeli thought in the post-Shoah world makes his work an especially interesting addition to this discussion (as we speak now in Haifa in the jubilee year of Israel's independence). Fackenheim's post-Shoah theology/philosophy also is developed in a radical departure from the phenomenological tradition represented by Heidegger. Fackenheim, in fact, argued through much of his work that no previous philosophy was adequate to shape an understanding of the Shoah. The radical nature of this claim has hardly yet been accepted for Fackenheim contends that all narratives -- religious or philosophical -- fail to help comprehend or give reason for the Shoah.[3] Since no ontology can accomplish understanding not even an effort to retrieve some meanings of the narratives can provide an adequate ontology, a way of thinking about the post-Shoah world. In this line of thinking Fackenheim is again radically postmodern in the same line as Levinas and Maccoby.

---

[3] Emil Fackenheim, "Holocaust and Weltanschauung: Philosophical Reflections as to Why They Did It," *Remembering for the Future,* Franklin Littell and Yehuda Bauer, ed. (Oxford: Pergamon Press, 1988), vol.II, pp. 1850-1862.

This rejection of ontology (it is not always so clear if Fackenheim has abandoned all effort to develop such an ontology, but his presentation at the same Oxford conference mentioned above does suggest that he has) leads Fackenheim to assertions that have become quite thoroughly identified with him.[4] First, he asserts that only one command holds absolute validity for the post-Shoah Jew, that no posthumous victory for Hitler be allowed. In essence this command means simply the necessity for Jewish survival. In fact, for Fackenheim this bare assertion of survival, which is not a new narrative but simple action to prevent Hitler from gaining posthumous achievement of any of Hitler's goals toward the Jews, is a relocating of Jewish identity from the past of Torah to only the present commanding voice to act. Indeed, Fackenheim argues that no redeeming voice but only a commanding voice remains after the Shoah, only the ethical and nothing of the ontological.

Still, this emphasis on mere survival, which is one form of an emerging self acting in response to the other is not the full picture of Fackenheim's vision. Instead, he does bring a theme out of the narrative of Israel's past (*tikkun olam*, to heal the world) to help understand the shape of this emerging self.[5] Thus, for Fackenheim the self is not a bare assertion of survival, what could be seen as an act of desperation, but emerges as a self like the self of Levinas, the self for the other emerging in acting. Ethics becomes the key, but an ethic of healing. And this healing is not rooted in a notion of a redeeming voice of the divine since that no longer can be heard, not even the narrative said, but a healing that is a response to the Shoah and to a post-Shoah world. Thus, if we apply this insight from Fackenheim in making more explicit the theme from Levinas, there is both a deconstructing and a reconstructing in this new paradigm for American post-Shoah theology. The deconstructing shatters previous identities and the reconstructing is of something new, a mending of the "world."

Bauman in Conclusion

In Fackenheim we already have an emerging a way of thinking that refuses to set up an either or but leaves the possibility of both/and in the two ways of thinking about postmodernity.

[4] The following positions can be found in Emil Fackenheim, *God's Presence in History* (New York: Harper and Row, 1970).

[5] Emil Fackenheim, *To Mend the World* (New York: Schocken Books, 1982).

Fackenheim sees both a full breaking of the narrative tradition (no redeeming voice) but yet the glimmer of continuing presence of at least a pre-rational sense of a tradition of mending the world that is surely an expression of a particular tradition. Thus, in Levinas we see an urging of the emergent moment that becomes the crucible for a new sense of self, a self that is responsible but only in the unsaid sense of finding the self in the other. For Fackenheim, there is this remnant self, perhaps even enough to satisfy Ricoeur's suspicion that there is a self out of which comes the sense of responsibility, even the minimal self that responds to a commanding voice.

This move to think of the postmodern as both/and is especially evident in the thought of Zygmunt Bauman and it is no surprise that Bauman draws heavily on Levinas. It is also no surprise that Bauman sees postmodern ethics as post-Shoah ethics and that this takes the shape I have already identified with a peculiarly European way of thinking about the Shoah. I still believe that the link between Levinas, Fackenheim and Bauman in the Jewish heritage is so significant not to be overlooked even if Fackenheim is the only one of the three who self-consciously identifies himself as a Jewish thinker. Bauman also sees that ethics and responsibility arises not from rationality **but from itself** following the lead of Levinas.[6] Thus, morality as such and responsibility in particular does not need a justification in reason, no narrative to give motivation. Bauman's appeal to Hannah Arendt emphasizes this even more as he uses her sense of the ethical as it appeared in the context of the Shoah as behavior completely understood in the context of acting often quite apart from expectations and social rationalities (morality, as he says, becomes an "insubordination towards socially upheld principles").[7]

My point all along has been to understand why accounting for European thinking on the Shoah is essential for any adequate American post-Shoah theology. My contention is that only in such a taking account does an American post-Shoah theology get put into the framework of postmodern thinking and that this link is peculiar to European thought. This means that a post-Shoah theology that accounts for the European perspective tends toward a deconstruction of particular identity (of Christian identity) in favor of a focus on the emergent responsible self in acting for the other. Theology becomes

---

[6] Zygmunt Bauman, *Postmodern Ethics* (Oxford: Balckwell, 1993), p. 249.

[7] ibid. Bauman, p. 249.

ethics, postmodern ethics. Even as I say that though, I have discovered that postmodern thought might be best understood as post-Shoah thinking in that the particular ideas of thinkers such as Levinas, Fackenheim and Bauman (Bauman perhaps especially) cannot be understood fully in any other way. In that way, applying the questions of post-Shoah thinking we come to understand why postmodern thought emerged and developed almost exclusively in Europe. But this means that we are finally left with yet a further move, that ethics implies social analysis both in terms of how the two intellectual communities (Christian and Jewish) respond differently and allow for different insights about the post-Shoah world. Such an analysis is likely to lead to even greater insight into post-Shoah European thought, into the difference between American and European post-Shoah theologies, into the distinctions between Jewish and Christian post-Shoah and postmodern thinking and into the potential shapes of post-Shoah theologies.

So let me conclude with Bauman who in using Anthony Giddens talks about our late modern age as an age of risks.[8] Of course, this can mean that risks are seen in relation to the social realities fashioned by a modern world and Bauman sees the Holocaust as the preeminent example of modern rationalities. In this way, our postmodern world can still act in a strange way by calculating the risks (by figuring scientific probabilities if you will). Such calculation would pretend to give rationale to moral action, or acting of any sort, but cannot give rise to moral acting in a post-Shoah, postmodern world. That is, if acting is essentially insubordination toward socially upheld principles (or as Fackenheim argues acting to mend the world), then risks in acting have to be seen as not calculated but taken even in spite of the odds. Thus, what is needed is a new paradigm for American post-Shoah theology that not only deconstructs identity, that not only reconstructs morality as a vision of mending the world that emerges in acting for the other, but risks a new social reality that cannot be predicted by probabilities but only is striven for in acting for the other, a reality that is itself emerging. Perhaps there will be a narrative that is shaped after the fact but it will not be a narrative like any that we have heard or maybe in the spirit of Bauman a narrative that is both like all that we have heard before and like none that we have heard before, a theology that only comes into being as we find ourselves most fully in affirming the other. This I believe is the hint of a post-Shoah theology that tries to take seriously European thought on the Shoah.

---

[8] ibid., Bauman, pp. 200-204.

Chapter 7: The Dialogical Connection: A Source for Ethics and Justice

After twenty years of awareness, new cases of HIV infection are increasing on the global scale (5.3 million new cases in 2000) and the new cases of HIV/AIDS are especially severe for Sub-Saharan Africa, Eastern Europe and Southeast Asia. Once more, we are experiencing a disturbing coincidence of newly virulent versions of the virus and increasing apathy in the general populations.[1] These three aspects of the current status of the HIV/AIDS pandemic are only a part of the full set of issues but enough to help us see that we urgently need new and adequate ethical models for the 21st century. They must now be both global in scope and able to account for the plight of the marginalized. They must also have the capacity to generate strategies of action that can effectively move large numbers of people to see the urgency of the issues we face.

The aim of this chapter is to explore one possible model for ethics that is based on the extraordinary insight of thinkers like Emanuel Levinas and Zygmunt Bauman, namely that ethics is rooted in a fundamental inter-subjective response to the other.[2] Of course, such a model must provide a corrective in that a response to the other can mean either a sensitivity and respect for the other or a calculated objectifying of the other as a means to some economic end (even if this is implicit and unintended).[3] I will suggest a model that I have called the dialogical connection. This connection actually involves three

---

[1] The statistics and information used in this paper are taken from the document *AIDS Epidemic Update: December 2000* of the World Health Organization (http://www.unaids.org/wac/2000/wad00/files/WAD_epidemic_report.htm)

[2] cf., Emanuel Levinas, "God and Philosophy," in *The Postmodern God*, Graham Ward, ed. (Oxford: Blackwell Pub, 1997), pp. 52-73), also *Totality and Infinity* (Pittsburgh: Duquesne Univ. Press, 1969); Zygmunt Bauman, *Postmodern Ethics* (Oxford: Blackwell Pub., 1993).

[3] Bauman, *Postmodern Ethics*, p. 244.

moments -- the dialogical intent, the emergence of dialogical community and the intentional and expanding inclusion of the marginalized. The paper begins with a brief summary of the view of Levinas concerning the ethical self.

Levinas

My development of Emanuel Levinas' view (which I believe is also adapted and accepted by Zygmunt Bauman) is not to assume that he has fully offered an adequate view of human existence or of the identity of the self but because his view presents a cogent understanding of the self that fits an evolutionary view of reality. For Levinas, the self has no essential form or presence since it comes into existence only in the encounter with the other which takes over any sense of individual identity. This is a radical form of inter-subjectivity that does not allow for any frozen present, any way to have a knowledge of an independent self; thus, this is a fully evolutionary self that comes into being and fades away at every moment of interaction with the other. There can be no pre-meditation in this idea of subjectivity, then, since the self is altered in each moment by the encounters with the other. The only ongoing factor is the "for-the-other" which is an expression of the realization that the self owes its existence to the other and requires the other for any real sense of subjectivity and responsibility. It is in this "for-the-other" that responsibility has meaning since both the self and the other emerge in our experience at the same time. Also, we can speak of transcendence only in the moment of the encounter that at once pulls beyond ourselves to the other and produces a new "self" in the process.

It is interesting that this sense of the self's being consumed by the other does not lead Levinas to existential absurdity as, for example, it does for Jean Paul Sartre for whom any action in this web of connections begins to lose either meaning or authenticity.[4] Each of these thinkers was dramatically influenced by the horrors of the Holocaust and their response determined by this very real/unreal world produced by the camps. But Levinas sees meaning emerging for us in the encounter with the other and in the ethical impulse of "acting for-the-other." Thus, Levinas believes that narratives of meaning are rationalizations after the fact but contends, nevertheless that there is a

---

[4] Cf., Jean Paul Sartre, *Being and Nothingness* (New York: Washington Square Press, 1953), especially part III, chapters 1 and 3.

real sense of ethical responsibility and meaningful action in the dialogical encounter.

This notion of the self is not essentialist in that there is no "self" that remains or is sustained outside of the moments of encounter. I believe, therefore, that the ever emerging self that Levinas describes fits nicely an evolutionary model of reality which also requires a constant ebb and flow of events produced by random encounters in the natural world including the human sphere of activity. For Levinas we cannot know the self by universal categories or by social context even though social context is the nexus of the formation of the evolutionary self.[5] The self is only known as emergent in this acting for the other. On the other hand, Levinas does not fully account for the information gained through such encounters, which I think becomes a part of each new moment of self-awareness even if the self is "itself" fleeting. Thus, Paul Ricoeur is probably right in his suspicion that there is a self-hiding in the bushes of this model, lurking all along.[6] But this is not a subjectivity, as Ricoeur would have it, but a reservoir of information that may or may not emerge along with the self in each new encounter.

The Model of Dialogical-Connection

I offer now a model for ethics that arises from my understanding of Levinas. The notion of "for-the-other" has for Levinas two different but at the same time coincidental components. First, this is true transcendence, for him, in that there is a sense of connection that enables us to see ourselves in the other, or rather in the encounter. This sense of connection is a reality that Levinas presupposes, a reality that is the foreground to any actual inter-subjectivity. Levinas is inclined to identify this transcendence with God, but this means that God emerges for us in the encounter. There is no God, no sense of God, that exists outside of these encounters, and

---

[5] To my knowledge, Levinas does not self-consciously develop a notion of an evolutionary self even though I am arguing that this would be possible given his views. If that were done, I think that this model of self would be different than other attempts which see the self as the focal point of an evolutionary process, such as, that presented by Mihaly Csikzentmihalyi in *The Evolving Self* (New York: Harper, 1993).

[6] Ricoeur is dubious about the claim of a purely emerging self. He asks, "Would the self be a result if it were not first a presupposition, that is, capable of hearing the assignment?" *Figuring the Sacred*, (Minneapolis: Fortress Press, 1995), p. 126.

the sense of God is essentially this connection (I have called this the dialogical connection) of "acting for-the-other."

The second aspect of "for-the-other" is the immediacy of the encounter itself. There is a particular sense of a particular other that begs for a particular kind of acting and ethical responsibility. Since the other in the other's particularity meets us in the encounter, each moment is different and new as each self emerges in the connection. But, I get the impression that these two aspects are really one for Levinas since there is no self prior to an encounter that can actually know or sense true transcendence (the pre-existing connection).

An ethical model as I am proposing is a reflection on these two components of the immediate experience of the dialogical encounter. That is, the model aims to understand human actions and interactions and project reasons for acting and/or not acting in general or particular ways. Both Levinas and Bauman argue that such theoretical models have limited sense for us precisely because they are rationalizations.[7]   If they cannot account for (1) the ground of responsibility in the sense of "for-the-other" and (2) the randomness of such encounters, they are also quite useless. This test of ethical systems threatens to undo most ethics since it threatens most understandings of universals. How can the ground for ethics be immediacy of encounter and be subject to radical randomness? This cannot be done unless we shape a model that begins with the dialogical encounter itself as fundamental.

Dialogical Intent

The encounter requires an initial intent that can be characterized once it emerges. There must be some tendency toward encounter of a specific sort for this notion of "for-the-other" to make any sense. This intent can be seen in two ways, again both of which seem to coincide in the moment of encounter. First, the intent is a product of the process of evolution itself. That is, our proclivity to meet the other in an encounter is imbedded in the long process of

---

[7] This is surely true for Levinas as any argument presenting reasons for imposes an ontology on the immediacy of acting and even covers over the reality of the testimony of this encounter as he argues in *Otherwise than Being* (Dordrecht: Kluwer, 1991). Bauman argues that morality remains irrational and cannot be universalized, thus implying the same that rationalizations not only come after the acting but distort the truth of the moment of moral encounter as for example he argues in *Postmodern Ethics*, pp. 12ff.)

connections that pre-date the emergence of human beings. If we recognize this, then we are led to see that there is already a significant history that we inherit in whatever social context we are located. This sense of proclivity (that meaning of intentionality) is, thus, more than our moment of encounter but is known in particular by each of us in the moment. We can know it no other way. My students in the Holocaust class, for example, are led to read materials that urge them into an encounter with information, people and realities that they had never before thought about. I can see in these students different levels of readiness for this encounter and theirs is not simply a conscious act but remains imbedded somewhere in their own histories of encounter, shaped by those encounters. This does not mean that a student who has traveled, for example, is more likely to be open than one who has not traveled, but there may be a tendency for greater openness when there is a reservoir of past contacts with different cultures and people. Of course, we now have increased contacts enormously by the Internet and can wonder if this will mean a more rapid evolution of the dialogical intent.

What this means is that despite the randomness of our individual encounters and our particular social context, there is an overall tendency toward dialogical connection within which we all participate. This may be the foundation of Levinas' claim that this is "poor ethical subjectivity deprived of freedom."[8] We are determined in this way by the flow of the process and the limits of these tendencies and the flow toward a larger sense of dialogical connection can be seen in the emergence of the many dialogues stretching across boundaries of identity that we are aware of around us.

The second sense of intention is in the acting itself. We actualize the tendency toward dialogue with the encounter and we continue to do so with each new encounter. This is intentional in the normal sense because "we" can choose to move toward dialogue or away from encounter. Again, my students in the Holocaust class encounter new ideas and material in this larger process that creates a climate of dialogue so that their choices seem more reasonable and acceptable if not inevitable. Within this set of choices, we can see an ever-widening set of encounters produced by an ever-forming dialogical intention.

As I said before, this intention can be characterized now by a set of senses of openness:

---

[8] Levinas, "God and Philosophy," p. 71.

(1) an openness to the other as other
(2) an openness to what the other discloses as having meaning and truth
(3) an openness to ourselves and a re-thinking of ourselves and our senses of meaning about our lives and the larger world and our view of truth
(4) an openness to risk change[9]

Of course, the last point in this set of opennesses is both a choice and simply a part of the larger tendency toward dialogical connection. What emerges as part of the dialogical intent is, however, the other as other, that is as having authentic reality for us encompassing the process of disclosure that now can become incorporated into my "self" as well, in whole or part. This disclosure and invitation to openness is what is required as an ethical premise for the notion of "for-the-other." It is also a guard against other forms of connection that are non-dialogical, such as Bauman notes when he says that the other can be treated "as a matter of accounts and calculations, of value for money, of gains and costs, of luxury one can or cannot permit."[10] Once the other is real for us and discloses for us herself, then we are not permitting the other to be in our awareness because the other has become us. This became clear to me years ago when a Rabbi teaching for our predominantly Christian university so moved the students that they could no longer see him as another, the other, but were moved to identify with him.[11] This is surely the process of dialogical connection.

Dialogical Community

---

[9] This model for dialogue was first developed in James F. Moore, "Team-Taught, In-Class Dialogue," in *Methodology in the Academic Teaching of Judaism,* Zev Garber, ed. (Lanham, MD: University Press of America, 1986), pp. 201ff., and further developed in a new way in James F. Moore, "Dialogue: an Infusion Method for Teaching Judaism," in *Academic Approaches to Teaching Jewish Studies,* Zev Garber, ed. (Lanham, MD: University Press of America, 2000), pp. 233ff. The model is explained in greater detail in each of these essays.

[10] Bauman, *Postmodern Ethics,* p. 244.

[11] An expanded discussion of this classroom experience can be found in Moore, "Team-Taught, In-Class Dialogue," pp. 205ff.

Dialogical intent can already imply an ethical model, something akin to what Paul Ricoeur calls an ethic of discussion.[12] In a sense the engagement does require rules and if this is actually dialogue, then those rules must be agreed upon. Various rules might be implied like the rule that all have the "right" to speak and that any claim requires at least an effort to make the claim reasonable (understandable). For Ricoeur, these rules require some general sense of debatability, communicability, in which some form of universal is assumed (a common sense of what ideas mean.) But this may not be such a formal occasion or such extended forms of disclosure and argument. Indeed, many of the issues that confound us today cannot wait for formal argumentation to be concluded with a consensus even if, as Ricoeur argues, there is an implicit agreement to accept the final judgment of the group for those who engage in discussion. Such consensus may never happen and may not be necessary.

What is not seen in this assessment of an implicit ethic of discussion is that the encounter itself is already creating community, not in the formal sense proposed by philosophers like John Rawls, who assume a sort of social contract agreement.[13] Thus, the dialogical ethic is not so much rule governed, not at least in the many momentary encounters, but is rather sensed in the linking "with-the-other." The "with-the-other" experience is an effect of "acting for-the-other." Thus, community (living and acting with others) emerges from the more immediate impulse to act "for-the-other." The more these encounters are extended, the more this sense of community develops. The immediate encounter and ethical impulse is more primary than the

---

[12] Cf., Paul Ricoeur, *The Just* (Chicago: University of Chicago Press, 2000), p. 118.

[13] This agreement is what Rawls calls "the original position," which is more a theoretical presupposition than a presumed actuality. See, John Rawls, *A Theory of Justice* (Cambridge, MA: Harvard University Press, 1971), pp.17ff. An extended discussion and critique of Rawls' position can be found in Ricoeur, *The Just*, pp. 36ff. The argument I am presenting has developed in my own thinking over the last 5 years and can be found I part in James F. Moore, "Re-Envisioning Christianity: A New Era in Christian Theological Interpretation of Christian Texts," *Cross Currents*, Volume 50:4, pp. 437ff. I also acknowledge that the notion has been explored by any number of others, for example, Norbert Wiley, "The Politics of Identity in American History," *Social Theory and the Politics of Identity*, Craig Calhoun ed., (Oxford: Blackwell Pub., 1994), pp. 139ff.

ethical rules, which also emerge from the encounter. Among these rules is most primarily a genuine respect for the other. For example, I can remember my impulse as a child to respond to any challenge against my brother. I cannot remember any point in time that an agreement was reached that I would do this or that my brother asked for it. This strong sense of loyalty, a full expression of respect, emerged from the process of encounter that happened on an ongoing basis with my brother. Just this last year, one of my longstanding partners in Jewish-Christian dialogue stated with force that he saw me now as a brother and had no doubt that I would be prepared to rescue him if we faced another Holocaust.

And now I return to the confounding issues of HIV/AIDS for a moment. I am convinced that we are able as individuals and as a society to dismiss the threat of the pandemic because we sense that it has subsided in the U.S. Now we ought to know that this is itself a fiction. But my point is that we are often isolated from encounters with the people of Sub-Sahara Africa who see that the effect of the spread of AIDS in their countries will be akin to the devastation felt in Medieval Europe as a result of the Plague. 25 million people in Sub-Sahara Africa are infected and 3.8 million new cases were reported there in just this last year.[14] The awareness of this crisis for my students increased dramatically this last year when a student from Africa chose to do research on the social issues affecting our ability to address the crisis in Africa. One face and one encounter allowed the students to see 25 million in human terms. Much the same happens with students who read narratives of survival from the Shoah and other genocides or sit face to face with a survivor.

The connection that becomes community is tenuous since we tend to act often in "self" interest unless we no longer can separate our interests from the interests of others around the globe. But the ethical sense arises from the encounter and in the encounter we gradually come

---

[14] The statistics and information used in this paper are taken from the document *AIDS Epidemic Update: December 2000* of the World Health Organization (http://www.unaids.org/wac/2000/wad00/files/WAD_epidemic_report.htm) The lengthy report also includes sections regarding the emergence of newly virulent and drug resistant strands of the virus and last year we saw again an increase in new cases in the U.S. while some efforts to combat health conditions in Sub-Sahara Africa as well as the likelihood that a majority of those in the highest risk group are already infected meant a downturn in the number of new cases in some areas.

toward a larger sense of community. Without the encounter such community sense will not arise. We can call this a dialogical community in that we are transported across the boundaries that separate us as other by the connection formed in such dialogical encounters to the point where boundaries no longer function in the same way. It is not that we see the humanity of others in this moment, for this is both arrogant and false. Humanity tends to be an abstracting term whereas the experience is immediate. It is perhaps, rather, we see humanity (or humaneness) in ourselves.

Dialogical Inclusion

Elinor Fuchs writes about the failure in reacting to the Bosnian crisis, "'Never again,' the single great moral victory to emerge from the defeat of European fascism, and in this sense the ethical core of twentieth-century humanist reconstruction, is finished now. It is has been 'historicized,' even if the West gathers itself to end the marriage."[15] Perhaps she is ready to dispense with moral victories since such ethical claims mean little. It was not so much that moral sensitivity was lacking in the failure of the nations to intervene on behalf of the Jews in the Shoah and, thus, never again is a cry not for more moral principles but for action. But one can hardly say with such confidence that we needed Bosnia to show us lost hope in human action. Surely we could have seen this already in Cambodia and East Timor if not also in Rwanda. The point is that any ethical system that is to mean anything must be more than principle and it must be more than simply communal sensitivity. The failure in Bosnia but even more critically in Rwanda was a failure to act despite the presence of both an ethical sense and an identification with the victims.

And to what extent are we now faced with an enormous challenge with the HIV/AIDS pandemic. The dialogical connection requires another stage, a stage of inclusion, that has at least the following components. First it must lead us to act with the other as part of our normal sphere of activity. Second, this must lead to strategies of action that enable us to respond before there is a greater consensus and even when there is no self-interest. First of all, it is surely already a part of the growing sense of community that we are prevented from losing sight of the humanity of the other. The other side of Fuchs'

---

[15] Elinor Fuchs, "Saving Bosnia (and Ourselves)," *Genocide, War, and Human Survival*, Strozier and Flynn, ed. (Lanham, MD: Rowan and Littlefield, 1996), p. 163.

argument has to be that we at least notice the need to act when there are signs of crisis. We are fully aware now that the crisis in Africa calls for a global network of action, but why now? Where was the sense of dialogical community to react to crises of at least equally far-reaching importance like the social and political systems that prevent the development of adequate health care or the spreading problem of contaminated water that means an infant mortality rate of 25-35%. These have been perennial problems not only in the nations of Sub-Sahara Africa but in other developing nations as well. The troubling fact is that our interest, such as it is, is likely tempered and dulled by both the lack of immediate danger to us and by a very real racial divide that influences both public and private reaction to such crises. We are now ready to act because, in part, we know that this disease can infect us. The challenge, however, is not just the enormity of the crisis but it is also the basic problem of whether we can act for the other even before or in situations beyond what is our immediate self-interest. It is possible that we see in this worldwide alert about HIV/AIDS just how far we have to go to create a global community peopled by selves prepared to act "for-the-other."[16]

Secondly, our ethical model requires a sensitivity that at once recognizes the role of global powers (economic and political) but also can foster local response networks that do not wait for actions by governments or by the UN. Paul Knitter argues for a globally responsible dialogue in which issues are seen on the scale (the global scale) that is appropriate for the crisis, but strategies are developed locally (in concert with global networks of action) to meet immediate issues.[17] This last point is what I am calling dialogical inclusion not so much as a conscious act of choosing to include the other but as the natural outgrowth of the connection itself. The dialogue creates a

---

[16] Any number of critical sources show the clear inter-linking of issues of health and social organization and abuse of power that are the wider context of the crises in Africa. Without a recognition of these wider issues, we can hardly act in responsible ways even with regard to the HIV/AIDS pandemic. Cf., James Glynn, Charles Hohm and Elbert Stewart, ed. *Global Social Problems* (New York: Harper-Collins, 1996), especially pp. 110ff. And Anthony Giddens and Mitchell Duneier, *Introduction to Sociology* (New York: W.W. Norton and Co., 2000), pp. 429ff.

[17] Paul Knitter, *One Earth, Many Religions* (Maryknoll, NY: Orbis Books, 1996), pp. 15ff.

reality that no longer allows inaction and with that requires an expanding inclusiveness in our acting.

Witold Gombrowicz, the philosophical Polish novelist and playwright brought this to life in his plays when he showed how we are not only shaped by those who are key players in our lives but also by those who appear on the margins.[18] This happens, of course, only in encounters that allow those on the margins to be identified with the emerging self, in the dialogical connection. This viewpoint is, perhaps, more optimistic about humanity than Gombrowicz would allow, but seems to be justified if we accept that the self emerges, as Levinas argues, in the dialogical connection, as a self acting for the other.

Several years ago I was involved in an effort by seminary students to cooperate with organizations in an American city. One evening we gathered to listen to some of the key social activists one of whom said that if we wanted to help, then we must choose to move to live in the inner city for a while and then we would be prepared to know how to act. The point made, I now realize, is not a matter of information but rather a matter of contact. An ethic built on the idea of a dialogical connection is finally one that creates an urgency for us that will not allow us to stay where we are but challenges us to move to another place. This is the urgency of the encounter, the urgency of being consumed by the presence of the other; the urgency built on the power of the connection that merges with our emerging selves, the dialogical connection.

---

[18] Cf., Ricardo Nirenberg, "Gombrowicz, or the Sadness of Form," *Of(f) Course: A Literary Journal*, Number 2, Fall/Winter, 1998. I am indebted to Dr. Barbara Strassberg for her insight, comments on this text and for introducing me to Bauman, Gombrowicz and any number of others who have informed and expanded my perspective.

Chapter 8: Christianity after the Holocaust and in the Twenty-First Century

Every credible Christian thinker who has attempted to respond to the Holocaust has, in some way, accepted the challenge that Irving Greenberg thrust before us now more than twenty years ago.[1] We understand that there is a link between Christian teaching in the past and the failure of Christians to intervene on behalf of Jews and other victims during the Holocaust. This failure requires all Christian responses to the Holocaust to be a reconsideration and revision of Christian teaching with the hope that this will never happen again. I and others have gone further to say with Greenberg that no theological statement can be made after Auschwitz that could not be made in the presence of the burning children.[2] This means that all theology after Auschwitz must be carried on in dialogue with Jewish partners at the very least and also must account for the memory of the burning children as an integral part of teaching about Christianity.

This goal of post-Shoah Christian theology and, hopefully, of post-Shoah Christianity is clearly idealistic. We must constantly recognize that a significant portion of the Christian community and many who call themselves theologians have done very little thinking about Christian teaching on the terms laid out above.[3] In addition, we

---

[1] Irving Greenberg, "Cloud of Smoke, Pillar of Fire..." in *Auschwitz: Beginning of a New Era?* Eva Fleischner, ed. (New York: KTAV, 1977).

[2] James Moore, *Christian Theology after the Shoah* (Lanham, MD: University Press of America, 1993).

[3] An earlier attempt to organize various thinkers can be found in, James Moore, "The Holocaust and Christian Theology: A Spectrum of Views on the Crucifixion and the Resurrection in the Light of the Holocaust," in *Remembering for the Future*, Franklin Littell and Yehuda Bauer, ed., (Oxford: Pergamon Press, 1988), vol. I, pp. 844-857.

recognize that key areas of Christian teaching that continue to repeat the travesties of the past are often communicated by teachers and preachers, many times without explicit intent through the conduct of regular worship practices and through Christian educational materials. Thus, we know that we have a long way to go before we have reached the aim of a credible post-Shoah Christian theology and teaching. It is a process that is on-going nevertheless.

Even so, we are also quite confident that the work that has been done has made an impact. A myriad of universities, often private Christian denominational schools, now have regular courses on the Holocaust which explicitly teach about Christian complicity and encourage students, particularly Christian students, to think about both the role of Christian teaching in influencing individual and group action as well as the potential for new ways of thinking to make a real difference for the future. We know that many have tried to revise Christian education materials so as to reflect a new attitude about how key ideas are taught, particularly Christian views of the Jewish people. Liturgies have been written and new hymns incorporated into worship which change the messages in both the regular worship services as well as special occasions like Good Friday and Easter. All of this has made a noticeable change so that we can hope, even if tentatively, that when people watch such programs as the recent mini-series "Uprising" they will be able to sort through the issues and understand the setting and know that this is a reflection of real events that were for the most part perpetrated by people confessing to be Christians. Even more, we hope that Christians have come to know Jews and the history of Jewish-Christian relations in such a way that they will act to denounce acts and words of hatred in any context they observe or in any situation that they can influence. This is clear evidence of a change in Christianity for the twenty-first century.

The Disturbing Signs

Having said all this in a very brief way, many of us are deeply troubled by other signs that show a picture opposite to our more positive even if realistic hopes. We might see this in an upswing in neo-Nazi and/or simply anti-Semitic groups who foster lies and distortions about the Holocaust as a way of undoing the work for positive change. We still find those willing to put forward pseudo-academic work that make revisitionist claims that harbor sinister goals and are groundless at any rate.[4] And these efforts are often made in the name of Christianity. What is especially disturbing for me is that often Christians fail to see these efforts as worth response. We are slow to counter the claims or challenge the right for these champions of lies to be heard as if they were legitimate academics. The additional activities of such groups to organize occasions of violence means that we have not really made much headway in some ways in assuring that the evils of Auschwitz will never again occur.

We also see that there is a climate in our current cultural scene that can at best be labeled a lethargy which shows itself in a belief that we are past these things and do not need to continue to study and think and be made to face the questions brought about by the Holocaust. There may be also a swing toward conservatism in many places that often links itself to notions of exclusivity and feeds on a paranoia that leads to xenophobia. Such a general mood encourages many to support draconian measures of eliminating those who are different, not like us, not willing to automatically fit our picture of the ideal American (or French or German). What is more worrisome is the potential for a greater degree of indifference to racist violence of the sort that we see at the center of Nazi ideology.

Of course, Americans and even particularly American Christians, are not alone in succumbing to this attitude. The end results are that we are not truly primed to respond to anti-Semitism or any other form of ethno-hatred with any speed and when we do we are often too late again to be able to head off the spread of ethnic violence before it is too strongly entrenched. We might be willing to see a light at the end of the tunnel simply by acknowledging that we do see hatred and do react to ethnic violence now while before we would often accept this as part of the way things are, many even believing the way things ought to be. But we should be troubled, those of us searching for a different sort of world, a different sort of Christianity for the new century because the events in the Sudan, Ethiopia, Bosnia, East Timor, Rwanda, Kosovo not to mention Northern Ireland or the Middle East remind us that Christians are often all too willing to follow ideologies of hate and follow to the extremes of genocide. And we wonder out

---

[4] A fairly good response to these revisionists among many efforts can be found in Franklin Littell and Irene Schur, ed., *In Answer* (West Chester, PA: Sylvan Pub, 1988.

loud how this can be barely a generation after Auschwitz.
Elinor Fuchs writes near the end of an essay on Bosnia:

> "'Never Again,' the single great moral victory to merge from the
> defeat of European Facism, and in this sense the ethical core of
> twentieth-century humanist reconstruction, is finished now. It has
> been 'historicized,' even if the West gathers itself to end the
> marriage."[5]

Her observation captures what many of us have felt regarding
the latter part of the twentieth century, that the claim that we will
prevent another Holocaust (Shoah) is surely countered by the ongoing
series of new genocides that seem only to repeat both the ideologies
and the failures of the past. It is this feeling that must form the
context for any current assessment of Christianity after the Shoah,
quite apart from any review of what has actually been written and done
as a response. This ethical core is certainly as much for Christianity
and for Christians the center-piece of all our responses to both the
horrific events of the Shoah and the disturbing response and/or lack of
response of Christians during the years of the Nazi onslaught. We
have made it our pledge to so re-think Christianity and Christian
teaching and action that the future must surely produce a better
response than the past and we must surely have made ourselves ready
to respond to every warning signal of a recurrence.

We would think that the last 50 years or so have done just
that, but too many new challenges confront us for us to be very
optimistic about what has really happened. Now, the events of
September 11th and after have raised for me, and I think for many
others who have dedicated themselves to the study of the Shoah and
what we can do about a post-Shoah Christianity, new and unnerving
evidence that we should be worried. Or must we simply join Fuchs in
lamenting our failures. I am inviting us to look closely at three key
factors that are troubling me at this point and through them see the
efforts of post-Shoah thinking and the dark clouds that now unsettle
us. First, we hoped to shape the religious traditions in such a way that

---

[5] Elinor Fuchs, "saving Bosnia (and Ourselves)" in *Genocide, War, and Human Survival*, Charles Strozier and Michael Flynn, ed. (Lanham, MD: Rowan and Littlefield, 1996), p. 163.

they could not be so easily co-opted by political leadership for political means. Second, we had hoped that we were attuned to the political use and abuse of religious language so as to intervene with a prophetic voice whenever such abuse would emerge. Third, we have been sure that we could and would in each new challenge be prepared to stand with the potential victim of abuse joining them in resistance to any power that would seek to target and eliminate any other people. Indeed, we have prided ourselves in at least this way that we now are able to espouse a Christianity that is fully open to accepting and embracing the other so that each new threat would automatically lead us to support those in danger no matter what our personal attitude may be about that other. These three points of a post-Shoah Christianity have been severely challenge over the last several weeks and I believe are what is at stake in the despair voiced by Elinor Fuchs.

Political Co-opting of Religion and the Abuse of Religious Language
          These three points are central to most responses by Christians to the Holocaust because we have assumed that if alerted to the failures of the past, Christians will act differently in the future. The point made so clearly by Franklin Littell over the years has been that we need a system of early warning signals that will trigger recognition that events are moving in the same direction as they did in Nazi Germany.[6] Indeed, we have been quite good at seeing those signals in many cases, but all this presumes that we are looking elsewhere, at someone else with a different ideology. We are alerted to think about the outside or fringe groups who threaten democratic freedom. We do not ordinarily see that we should be alert to signals given by the leaders of our democracy.
          I am not sure why we would think this way since much of the work by Christians after the Shoah has focused on the question of Christian anti-Semitism and what Jules Isaac first labeled a "teaching of contempt."[7] Thus, we have been made fully aware that religion and religious leaders are no guarantee against genocidal ideology. Quite

---

[6] Franklin Littell, "Essay: Early Warning," *Holocaust and Genocide Studies*, 4:483-90, 1988.
[7] Jules Isaac, *The Teaching of Contempt* (New York: Holt, Rinehart and Winston, 1964).

the opposite has been made apparent by many such as Clark
Williamson and Rosemary Ruether, that Christianity has from the
outset carried and taught the seeds for Jew hatred and for violence
against the one who is different.[8] All of this history of Christian
response, especially since the mushrooming of the various dialogues
between Christians and Jews since the late 1960's, intended to head
off a future abuse of religion and religious institutions for the sake of
promoting a particular political ideology, a step toward the institution
and the justification of violent action "against our enemies."

Of course, we have also seen that whatever small effort some
have made to radically change Christian thinking, the results are
hardly fully promising on the global setting. The records seem to
show that Christian leaders, even clergy, were responsible directly for
genocidal promotion and acts in both Bosnia and Rwanda. We might,
even while we are appalled by this, say that surely these actions were a
product mostly of ethnic hatred and emerged in areas ripe for
vengeance and places where little impact of the post-Shoah dialogue
was felt. And the violence that Christians perpetrate elsewhere (in
Northern Ireland, Ethiopia, Israel, the USA, etc.) could be seen as
more representative of a surge of ethnic violence and long standing
issues than any result of Christian teaching as such. Besides, even in
the midst of the sort of despair felt so strongly by Elinor Fuchs, we are
inclined to take hope that people everywhere are quicker to see
injustice and act even if so poorly as with the various cases in Africa,
especially in Rwanda.

I am, however, deeply troubled by two features of recent
events that show how easy our alertness to these early warning signals
can be circumvented. To be sure, we are justified in identifying the
potential destructiveness of terrorist organizations and of regimes of
terror such as the Taliban. This presence of a legitimate concern is
hardly new to the horizon no matter how much we might point to
September 11th as a unique water shed event. The abuses in
Afghanistan were present already years before the World Trade Center
disasters and the terror networks we now wage war against in a new
way have been the subject of countless similar efforts to wage war if
not so openly identified as such. None of this is particularly new to

---

[8] Clark Williamson, *When Jews and Christians Meet* (St. Louis, CBP Press,
1988).

many around the globe as well, certainly not those in Israel or in East
Timor or in Cambodia or the Congo or the United Kingdom. If this
were a warning signal of these proportions, why then were we not
alerted to this earlier and why not react with the same intensity
earlier? We might imagine that we know the answers to these
questions, but we must honestly admit that this battle is not especially
new or even more intense now. It is simply closer to home for most
Americans.

        Thus, we should be alert to terror, but this is not my point
here. The point is that almost instantaneously with the cataclysm of
9/11 we heard this battle described in religious terms. Of course, we
succumbed to the language of the terrorists themselves and used the
same in response. They are evil and are intent on global domination
with secret plots to undermine our way of life. That these words were
tempered a bit after some concern attributed to the American Muslim
community does not seem to change the basic way that "our enemies"
are described consistently and continuously by our political leadership
and there is no one prepared, it seems, to challenge this use of
language. Naturally this is not the first time we (Americans) have
talked this way, but that we would construct a global policy by using
this sort of religious-like language is more than troubling.[9] And that
our leaders talk about the total annihilation of the enemy is chilling to
anyone who has spent time teaching the Holocaust. And, of course,
we presume that we are fully justified in speaking this way since our
cause is just.

        Are we not alarmed that our politicians were much quicker in
passing sweeping changes in the laws to hand over unencumbered
police power to law enforcement officials, especially federal law
enforcement, than they have been ready to pass airport security
legislation? We are more worried about increased federal bureaucracy
in hiring security screeners at check-in lines than we are openly
funding an increased domestic investigation of anyone who even
appears to be suspicious to law enforcement (even if they are guilty of
a traffic violation) and we are recruited as accomplices alerting the
authorities anytime we notice something suspicious. Am I making the

---

[9] See the opening essays in *Genocide, War, and Human Survival*, Charles
Strozier and Michael Flynn, ed. (Lanham, MD: Rowan and Littlefield, 1996),
as a comparision in the way dropping the bomb was handled.

point? And how is it that those who have spent so much energy teaching about the Holocaust have not been immediately crying for caution about this?

Instead, it was obvious to me that religious leaders were much quicker in readiness to gather for official functions of patriotism, for prayer vigils and joint services. I would rejoice in this sudden appearance of cooperation between Christian, Jewish, Muslim, Sikh and Hindu clergy if I did not see that the result is to promote the notion that we are all after all good patriotic Americans. To decide not to follow this path is to become a suspect. Of course, I will accept that for now we live in a society that is ready to tolerate the most divergent of views. Indeed, this is likely why terrorist organizations have found it so easy to use the U.S. as a base for operations. But there is a very troubling message projected when religious leaders presume that dialogue means fundamentally confessing together our Americanness and repeating phrases that reflect the attitudes of the political leadership. And this message has not been lost on the general public if my students are representative at all of this.

It is this very phenomenon that we have said repeatedly must not happen again. And I am not so naïve as to think that we can prevent such uses of religious ideas in a climate so prone to it. The point is not that political leaders are so willing to use religion for political purposes especially when they believe their cause is righteous and religious language will serve to motivate the masses to an emotional support. This is politics as we are becoming used to politics. The issue is how easily the great majority of religious leaders can be manipulated to support this political maneuver without any question whatsoever. I cannot hear the questions of my students when they ask how could Christians be led to so blindly follow the Nazis without seeing how easy it is for this to happen here. And we are ready to pay more, accept more surveillance and the fervor of finding and eradicating those responsible is riding high without any significant voice of caution from the religious communities.

The Protection of Potential Victims

This impact on religious communities and their leadership is reminiscent of the factors influencing bystanders of various genocides. The point is not one of indifference but rather the opposite, a clear sense of righteousness linked to patriotism. But this is hardly collaboration in the normal sense and we are not so much ready to make false comparisons with the Nazi era. The concern is the realization that religious communities are so easily manipulated and co-opted. On the other hand, the post-Shoah experience has led to another sort of reaction that is almost the opposite, a urgency to intervene, that also impacts the religious response.

The post-Shoah era has made us realize that any notion of never again requires the willingness to intervene before genocide occurs. This seems to be a central religious obligation for many but unfortunately in reality gets played out in a different way. Religious organizations are seldom the means for intervention in such instances which means that religious people are left to rely on governments for intervention and to a lesser extent the many humanitarian organizations. The problem with both in recent memory, be that in Bosnia or in Rwanda, was that such intervention is fraught with issues of political interest and/or unclear information about who needs our intervention. The Rwanda case is especially damning in that we were slow to act principally because of the backlash from a similar intervention in Somalia and also because of political ties that bound some governments in strange alliances. But when we did act, through governmental policy and the work of humanitarian organizations (including the work of the United Nations and the Red Cross), we found ourselves aiding the refugee murderers from Rwanda who left after they had essentially wiped out the Tutsi population. There is little guarantee that religious communities are able to effectively judge such cases until long after the fact because of misinformation during the events.

Of course, we are able to see some voices crying out in opposition, most recently it was at least encouraging that PBS and Bill Moyer gave Robert J. Lifton a chance to respond to the current crisis with a voice of reason. What is most obvious to us as well is that in the Gulf War and in this conflict with the Taliban, the government feels fully justified in limiting and even couching information fed to the media, our sole source for news for the most part. It is, thus, likely that we are again left with little choice but to support the effort, it seems, or appear to be supporting the Taliban. This sort of black and white treatment of issues can lead to disaster as has often been the case in the past for the U.S. Still, the cry from religious leadership has been essentially muted and the end result is that an extended conflict may well lead to the deaths of thousands if not millions of civilians whose only crime is that they happen to live in Afghanistan.

In the meantime we increase the likelihood that extreme elements in our own culture will not clearly divide the populations seeing that there is an ever greater need to isolate and to exclude any people in our nation who appear in someone's mind to be suspicious. Can we honestly expect that religious communities are prepared to prevent violence against unprotected minorities in this sort of political climate? Yes we can presume this but the model is finally clear to us. The interventionist model in which we take the role of resistor from the outside is so difficult to judge and so easily leads to political manipulation that this model cannot work. Instead, if resistance is the key for us it must be a resistance to any form of speciation (to use Erik Erickson's term)[10] that aims to divide the globe in black and white, good and evil, just causes and injustice. If we find ourselves co-opted into this speciational process we will not be able to avoid the trap of using religious ideas, arguments and power to justify violence against "the other."

Another Model – The Rescuer

I am led to see more than ever now that the model I suggested seven years ago as the working model for post-Shoah Christians is now the most credible model for our acting, the rescuer.[11] Let me briefly suggest, however, that this model is not only credible as a model for individual action though I am more and more convinced that the real test comes most often as individual choices and actions. The model makes sense in addition as a way of thinking about Christianity after the Shoah and into the twenty-first century.

I am thinking about the model as portrayed in the profiles of altruism as, for example, given to us by the Oliners.[12] First, we recognize the obvious and that is that rescue and the character of the rescuer is shaped and motivated by a variety of not always consistent factors. We avoid thinking of concerted action as such as if every moment requires the same response or every responder the same profile. Pluralism even in this model is still an important reality and

---

[10] *Genocide, War, and Human Survival*, Charles Strozier and Michael Flynn, ed. (Lanham, MD: Rowan and Littlefield, 1996).

[11] James Moore, *Christian Theology after the Shoah* (Lanham, MD: University Press of America, 1993).

[12] Samuel Oliner and Pearl Oliner, *The Altruistic Personality* (New York: Free Press, 1988).

ideal to recognize and protect. Second, we do have some elements of the narratives of Holocaust rescuers that help us see critical factors that must shape our future response to genocide. The rescuers for one thing were often people who were on the fringes of political power. To be disconnected from the interests of those who have social and political power is, in this case, an advantage. Also, rescuers were often convinced that they had to act simply because it was the right thing to do. But notice this sense of urgency to act, even a spontaneous response, is acting to save, to stand with, by and for those in danger of political oppression. It is a standing against, in that way, the political forces that would divide us into those worth saving and those already condemned. It is, of course, a principle in this way that we stand against these dividing efforts no matter what the proclaimed cause or who it is that aims to do this. In addition, rescuers often found that they had less to risk than others (impact, for example, on their livelihood or on those related or connected to them.) The principle at work here is similar to the one just enunciated, that we cannot presume that our interests are overridingly to protect our own but need to be able to see "the other" as our own.

Finally, the rescuer is often one who has the experience with the other in the past that has already changed an attitude that difference means separation. Indeed, often the ones rescued were friends, neighbors, colleagues. Of course, as with the other factors, such a profile hardly guarantees the act to rescue. Many who shared these qualities simply did not act. Still, we see that those who are already in some ongoing relationship with those who are from different communities, cultures, religions, races, classes will more likely count anyone from that group as part of their own group. Thus, I continue to declare that dialogue is critical to the continuing credibility of Christianity after Auschwitz.   Dialogue, Dialogue, Dialogue!!! Crossing boundaries breaks down boundaries and enables us to hear the other and see different sides to all issues. A Christianity that is devoid of dialogue, that simply crawls back into a protective shell of like minded people, will be a dead Christianity and will fail, most assuredly, to meet the challenge that Irving Greenberg set before us. I would prefer that Christianity as an institution die and that cells of dialoguers thrive for this is the only way toward any true realization of the notion of "never again."

But this is a struggle, a thousand year struggle even. I do not quickly see that Christianity has achieved a level of real credibility yet.

Indeed, we are continually challenged to fall back into the past and with each retreat to lose the battle to be genuinely Christian. But this process is going on and is making headway and will finally rise up and challenge every effort to divide us as human and not quite fully human. It is a challenge that we must not shrink from because we know that those who would want to co-opt the religious spirit for destructive, even genocidal, purposes are also tenacious.

INDEX

A

Fackenheim, Emil, 5, 28, 56, 70,
73-75, 85, 96, 97, 99, 109, 110
Fasching, Darrell, 27, 28, 35, 93
Future, 5, 32, 100, 102, 109, 125

G

Garber, Zev, 3, 9, 10, 118
Genocide, 9, 87, 121, 128, 129,
131, 134
Genesis, 26, 39, 51, 52, 61, 62, 65,
66, 68-71, 90, 93
Gentile, 28, 36, 38, 44, 53
Gentiles, 27, 28, 31, 39, 41, 48,
51, 53
God, 4; 6, 8, 9, 16, 18-21, 26, 28-
35, 37-40, 42-46, 49, 50, 52-
54, 56, 58, 61-71, 73-76, 78,
80-82, 84, 87, 88, 96, 97, 110,
113, 115, 117
Greenberg, Irving, 4, 15, 20, 34,
36, 56, 69, 70, 91, 93, 101,
125, 135

H

Haas, Peter, 94
Holocaust, 4, 5, 16, 17, 20, 30, 32,
34, 53, 67, 70, 75, 77, 81, 84,
87, 91, 99, 106, 109, 112, 114,
117, 120, 125-129, 131, 132,
135
Holy, 42
Humanity, 121

I

Imagination, 108
Interpretation, 24, 87, 92, 101, 119
Isaac, 8, 16, 27, 61-64, 66-68, 70,
78, 88, 100, 129
Isaiah, 43, 44

Israel, 26, 28, 30-33, 38, 51, 52,
55, 63, 66, 73-85, 109, 110,
130, 131

J

Jacob, 8, 22, 52, 93
Jesus, 10, 19, 21, 22, 24-26, 30-
33, 35, 36, 38, 39, 41, 44, 45,
47-49, 51, 53, 55, 56, 58, 62,
64-66, 68-70, 87, 89, 92, 102,
108
Jew, 10, 13, 15, 16, 18-20, 22, 25,
27-31, 33, 35, 36, 38, 39, 41,
44, 45, 47-49, 51, 53, 55, 56,
58, 61, 73-77, 79-84, 93, 97,
99, 102, 103, 105-107, 110-
112, 118, 120, 125, 126, 130,
132
Jewish, 10, 15, 16, 18-20, 22, 25,
27-31, 33, 35, 36, 38, 39, 41,
44, 45, 47-49, 51, 53, 55, 56,
58, 61, 73-77, 79-84, 93, 97,
99, 102, 103, 105-107, 110-
112, 118, 120, 125, 126, 132
John, 26, 61, 62, 64-67, 69-71, 87,
88, 96, 102, 119
JOB, 81
Justice, 113, 119

L

Land, 80
Law, 22, 25, 26, 28, 41, 44
Levinas, Emanuel, 91, 113, 114
Leviticus, 51
Life, 1
Littell, Franklin, 14, 20, 57, 100,
102, 109, 125, 127, 129

M

About the Author

James Moore is a professor in the Department of Theology at Valparaiso University and the Director for Inter-faith Programs for the Zygon Center for Religion and Science. He is author of *Sexuality and Marriage* (Augsburg Publishing, 1987), *Christian Theology after the Shoah* (UPA, 1993) and *Post-Shoah Dialogues* (UPA, 2004). He has authored numerous articles on Jewish-Christian relations, Holocaust education, and post-Shoah theology and is a member of the advisory boards for the Studies in the Shoah series at UPA, the Center for Holocaust, Genocide and Human Rights and the Wyman Institute.

CPSIA information can be obtained at www.ICGtesting.com
Printed in the USA
LVOW13s2331090114

368850LV00001B/218/P